Homer's *Odyssey*

A Study Guide for A Level

Athena Critical Guides

Table of contents

Homer's *Odyssey*: A Study Guide for A Level

Homer's *Odyssey*: A Study Guide for A Level

This study guide will assist you in your studies of Homer's *Odyssey*.

At the time of writing several UK examination boards offer A Level examinations in Classical Civilisation. One popular and key part of these examinations is the study of Greek and Roman epic, including Homer's *Iliad* and *Odyssey* as well as Virgil's *Aeneid*.

The works of Homer were considered by the Ancient Greeks to be the cornerstone of their culture and Homer's poetry remains an important foundation for modern literature. Homer's epic poems possess a unique composition, and the exciting tales of gods and heroes that they contain form an excellent starting point for the exploration of the ancient world and classical civilisation.

The aims and objectives of Advanced Level GCE in Classical Civilisation include;

- Develop an interest in and enthusiasm for Classical Civilisation and develop an understanding of the intrinsic value and significance of Epic Poetry.

- Acquire an understanding of different identities within society and an appreciation of aspects such as social, cultural, religious and ethnic diversity, as appropriate.

- Build on your understanding of the past through experiencing a broad and balanced course of study.

- Improve as an effective and independent learner.

- Develop the ability to ask relevant and significant questions about the past and to research these questions.

- Acquire an understanding of the nature of ancient literature and poetry.

- Develop your use and understanding of literary terms, concepts and skills.

- Make links and draw comparisons within and/or across different kinds of literature and thematic aspects.

- Organise and communicate your knowledge of Epic poetry and understanding in different ways, arguing a case and reaching substantiated judgements.

Studying GCE Classical Civilisation

This study guide has been written to provide a rewarding experience for those who are, or are interested in, studying Classical Civilisation. In particular, this study guide will assist you in understanding and examining the subject matter of epic poetry; Homer's *Odyssey*.

Who is this study guide for?

This study guide is intended to offer a satisfying experience for those learners who undertake an AS or A level qualification in Classical Civilisation. This qualification pathway is offered by AQA, OCR and CIE examination boards. This resource is primarily designed to assist those who are studying this topic for a Classical Civilisation qualification.

This study guide will help to lay a sound foundation for those who go on to study the Ancient World at a higher (degree) level as well as appeal to those who are interested in learning more about the ancient world generally and in particular, the epic poetry of Homer.

Please note that this study guide is not endorsed by the examination boards and as such is not an officially recognised product by AQA, OCR or CIE examination

Examination Boards offering study in Classical Civilisation

This product is designed to be used as a study aid in order for learners to attain a qualification in the following examination units;

OCR Examination Board

- Advanced Level GCE in Classical Civilisation

(H408/11) The World of the Hero

CIE Examination Board

- Advanced Level GCE in Classical Civilisation

(9274) Component 4: Gods and Heroes: the importance of epic

AQA Examination Board

- Advanced Level GCE in Classical Civilisation (2020): Component 2: CIV2B

*Please note that the AQA A level is an outgoing specification

that is not being replaced*

How to use this guide

This A Level study guide has been organised in such a way so as to help an A Level student of Classical Civilisation more easily understand the *Odyssey* and also to correspond to the major topic areas identified by the major examination boards.

To this end this Athena Critical Guide is divided into multiple **Parts** each containing four of five **sections** that relate to the overall theme of the relevant Part. Each subsection discusses a specific aspect or series of related aspects relevant to the A level student, so for example Part Two covers the background to Homer and introduces his techniques and each section deals with a specific aspect as identified below;

Part Two: The Telemachy

2.1 Xenia in the Odyssey

2.2 Book One: Athena inspires Telemachus

2.3 Book Two: The Ithacan debate: style and realism

2.4 Book Three: Nestor

2.5 Book Four: Menelaus and story telling

Each section is introduced with a number of bullet points that will help the reader to identify the focus of the section and also to help correlate the section to their relevant examination specification.

Within each subsection are a number of tasks and activities as well as glossary terms and additional points of information that are considered useful to an A Level student.

The tasks and activities are based on the structure and duration of questions posed by the examination boards therefore it is envisaged that they will be especially valuable in aiding the reader to prepare for their respective examinations.

Which translation of the *Odyssey* should I use?

This study guide does not recommend a specific translation of the *Odyssey*. No specific edition or translation of a text is set because of copyright availability issues in different parts of the world.

> *According to examination boards such as OCR and CIE, A level and AS level learners sitting the A Level examination in Classical Civilisation may use any translation of the text.*

However where a translation is printed on an OCR examination question paper two versions will be provided, these will be taken from:

- *Homer, 'Odyssey' translated by E. V. Rieu, revised translation by D. C. H. Rieu (Penguin)*
- *'Homer: Odyssey – The Wanderings of Odysseus', translated by A.S. Kline, online at http://www.poetryintranslation.com*

These are excellent translations and readily available to learners.

Another excellent translation is;

- Homer, *Odyssey. Translated by R. Fagles, Viking Penguin, 1996.*

Free versions of the Odyssey can be obtained from;

The Perseus digital Library; *www.perseus.tufts.net*

Kindle and iBook versions

Both Kindle and iBook versions may also offer free or purchasable versions of the *Odyssey* which are translated by different academics which may be used accompany this critical study guide.

Athena/ Athênê: A note on Greek names

Throughout this study guide it will be noticed that sometimes the Greek Goddess 'Athena' is mentioned, at other times the Greek Goddess 'Athene' is mentioned.

The original Greek for this Goddess is 'Athene', and the translator of the set text has used this spelling throughout his translation of the *Odyssey*. However, the more commonly encountered spelling is Athena and it is this version that is used in this guide. For this reason Latinised versions of Greek names will be used.

So; for example 'Kirké' will be reproduced as 'Circe' and 'Odusseus' as 'Odysseus'.

Dramatis Personae in the *Odyssey*

There are a lot of characters in the Odyssey and if this is the first time that you have studied the *Odyssey* it can get a little confusing remembering who is who. Below is a selection;

❖ **Olympian Gods**

Athena – Goddess of crafts and war, patron of Odysseus

Hermes- Messenger of the Gods and sometime helper of Odysseus

Poseidon – The Sea God whom Odysseus has angered

Zeus – Father of the Gods

❖ **Minor Gods**

Aeolus – God of Winds

Ino – A water Nymph

Calypso – Nymph that imprisons Odysseus for seven years

Circe – A witch who turns some of Odysseus' men into pigs but later helps

❖ **Ithacans**

Odysseus – the 'Hero' of the Odyssey

Penelope – the wife of Odysseus

Telemachus – Odysseus' son

Halitherses – An Ithacan and prophet

Eupeithes – father of Antinous

Irus/Arneaus – a beggar

Laertes – Odysseus' father

❖ **Servants at Odysseus' Palace**

Eumaeus – Loyal swineherd

Eurycleia – Penelope's maid and loyal servant

Eurynome - Penelope's maid and loyal servant

Melanthius – A disloyal goatherd

Philoetius – A loyal cowherd

Medon – a Herald

Phemius – a bard

❖ **Suitors**

Amphonius

Antinous

Eurymachus

Leodes

Amphimedon

❖ **Heroes and allies of Telemachus**

Nestor – King of Pylos

Peisistratus – son of Nestor

Menelaus – King pf Sparta

Helen – Queen of Sparta

Theoclymenus – a seer who seeks sanctuary

❖ **Opponents encountered during the *Odyssey***

Charybdis – A gigantic whirlpool

Cicones – A people Odysseus attacks

Laestrygonians – Giant cannibals

Polyphemus – A Cyclops

Scylla – Monster that consumes some of Odysseus' men

❖ **Phaeacians**

Alcinous – The king of the Phaeacians

Arete – Queen of the Phaeacians

Demodocus - Bard

Nausicaa – Phaeacian princess

❖ **The Dead Heroes and inhabitants of the Underworld**

Agamemnon

Achilles

Ajax

Heracles

Anticleia – mother of Odysseus

Note: There are many more characters in the *Odyssey*. It may be useful to create a reference guide of these characters.

Part One:

Homer and the *Odyssey*

Part One: Homer and the *Odyssey*

1.1 Homer's *Odyssey*

1.2 The Oral tradition of Homer's *Odyssey*

1.3 Linguistic and stylistic techniques in Homer's *Odyssey*

1.4 Shaping meaning: The Homeric Simile

1.5 The Homeric Hero

1.1 Homer's *Odyssey*

In this section we will;

- *Understand what we do and do not know about 'Homer'*

- *Begin to explore the structure and synopsis of the Odyssey*

- *Begin to consider the oral tradition and the textual transmission of the Odyssey*

Homer the poet

Homer is a shadowy semi-historical figure about which even the Ancient Greeks could not agree. His birthplace, date of birth and even (in more recent times) gender have all been disputed along with whether or not Homer was blind or not, or able to write or not.

Very, very little can be said with any degree of certainty, beyond stating that the Ancient Greeks believed that there was a poet called Homer who is credited with creating the epic poems of the *Iliad* and the *Odyssey* among others.

Conventional, modern dating places Homer as having lived *circa* 750-700 BC, and identifies him as either being born, or living in, one of several possible Greek cities along the coast of Asia Minor, the western sea-board of Turkey.

Homer was clearly removed in time from the legendary events about which he describes. It is safe to say that Homer was not a historian and was not concerned with recording actual, historical events. Tradition and attempts by some archaeologists have attempted to associate Homer's poems and the towns and societies of which he speaks with sites and finds dating back to the Mycenaean period of Greece.

However, it must be said that despite this Homer and the Bronze Age sites discovered by archaeologists such as Schliemann and Arthur Evans at 'Troy', Mycenae and Knossos are inextricably linked in the popular mind. In fact Homer comes from a period much later than these sites. Homer's world should be more accurately associated with the Greece of the 7-8th centuries BC. This is because many 'non-Mycenaean' elements can be identified in Homer's poems, which are clearly an intrusion from Homer's contemporary world (that of the Greek Dark Age) and stand at odds with many of the things we know about the earlier Mycenaean period.

Who wrote the *Odyssey* and the *Iliad*?

So far we have assumed that the author of both the *Iliad* and *Odyssey* was an individual poet called 'Homer'.

It has been assumed that;

- One individual created both works.

- This individual went by the name 'Homer'.

- The *Iliad* and the *Odyssey* were created in that order.

- The *Iliad* and the *Odyssey* were first performed between the 8th and 6th century BC.

- That these works were called '*Iliad*' and the '*Odyssey*'.

- That 'Homer' was a man.

In fact, all of these are just that; assumptions. However, none of these assumptions can be argued to be definitely accurate due to the great age of the works we are dealing with.

The Ancient Greeks certainly believed that there was one, sole author of both works, and the tradition has also painted this man as being called 'Homer', a blind bard whose birth has been claimed by at least seven cities states.

Modern academics have pointed out inconsistencies in both the *Iliad* and the *Odyssey* which suggest that different parts of both works come from different times and from different poets. For example, in the *Iliad* book 10, the Greek heroes Diomedes and Odysseus steal and ride horses away from the Thracians they have just raided. Everywhere else in both works horses are used exclusively to pull chariots. They are never ridden. Another example often used by academics seeking to identify different poets writing at different times is the rather odd ending of the *Odyssey*, book 24 of the *Odyssey* seems an addition, an appendix to the whole, and a rather disappointing one at that.

However, though there remain enough links and similarities between the two works that it is certainly still a possibility. It seems likely enough that even if the author of the *Odyssey* did not himself

---

A very approximate timeline for Homer

1600-1100 BC: approximate dates between which Mycenaean civilisation flourished.

850 BC: approximate date of the life of Homer given by Herodotus.

850-750 BC: many modern estimates place the creation of the oral versions of the *Iliad* and *Odyssey*

750 BC: earliest probable date of the '*pithekoussai cup*' – which is inscribed with lines from Homer.

750-650 BC: Likely date for the first written versions of the *Iliad* and the *Odyssey*.

---

compose the *Iliad*, he certainly knew about it in enough detail to reproduce much of its flavour and linguistic style in his own work.

It has often been argued that both the *Iliad* and the *Odyssey* could have been composed not by a single individual; instead, the argument runs that these are the work of a group of loosely associated poets who collaborated and updated these works to produce many variants which were in turn written down and codified into 'one' definitive version which survived down to 1488 when a manuscript of Homer was first printed in Italy.

Despite the strength and plausibility of these kinds of arguments, many academics prefer the theory that both the *Iliad* and the *Odyssey* were created by one individual called Homer. The simple truth is that given our lack of firm evidence one way or another; *we simply do not know*. The argument continues, and will probably continue for some time to come without a definitive answer.

A brief synopsis of the *Odyssey* is as follows;

The name *Odyssey* comes from the Greek *'Odusseia'* which means *'The story of Odysseus'*.

Aristotle in his *Poetics* explains the plot of the *Odyssey* as follows;

"A certain man has been abroad many years; he is alone and the god Poseidon keeps a hostile eye on him. At home the situation is that suitors for his wife's hand are draining his resources and plotting to kill his son. Then after suffering storm and shipwreck, he comes home, makes himself known, attacks the suitors; he survives and they are destroyed."

The *Odyssey* is 12,109 lines long and composed in hexameter verse. The first 'modern' printed version was issued in 1488 in Florence. It is from this printed version that modern translations are based.

The Ancient Greeks had a standardised version, with some variations. Evidentially some written copies were in circulation by the 6th century BC. These versions were used for public recitals at Athens and other Greek cities from the 6th century onwards. The different versions of the *Odyssey* and the *Iliad* were consolidated at Alexandria by the 3rd century BC.

The structure of the *Odyssey*

The *Odyssey* is an epic poem divided into 24 Books, covering a period of almost 10 years.

Book One	The Olympian gods determine it is time for Odysseus to return. Telemachus is inspired by Athena to seek news of his father.
Book Two	Telemachus leaves Ithaca, accompanied by a disguised Athena.
Book Three	Telemachus arrives at Pylos and meets Nestor.
Book Four	Telemachus journeys to Sparta and meets Menelaus.
Book Five	Hermes visits Calypso and instructs her to let Odysseus leave her island.
Book Six	Odysseus arrives on the island of the Phaeacians and meets Nausicaa.
Book Seven	Odysseus is well received at the palace of King Alcinous.
Book Eight	Demodocus tells tales of Troy causing Odysseus grief.
Book Nine	Odysseus begins telling the story of his *Odyssey*. Adventures among the Cicones, the Lotus eaters and the Cyclops.
Book Ten	The Odyssey continues, Odysseus encounters Aeolus the wind-god, the Laestrygonians and Circe.
Book Eleven	Odysseus journeys to the Underworld.
Book Twelve	Odysseus listens to the Sirens, narrowly escapes Scylla and Charybdis before his ship and men are killed after eating the cattle of the Sun.
Book Thirteen	Odysseus arrives home to Ithaca.
Book Fourteen	Odysseus meets Eumaeus and learns about the Suitors in his home.
Book Fifteen	Telemachus returns home from Sparta and goes to Eumaeus.
Book Sixteen	Odysseus is revealed to Telemachus.
Book Seventeen	Odysseus arrives back at his palace, disguised as a beggar.
Book Eighteen	Odysseus fights another beggar and Penelope announces she will remarry.
Book Nineteen	Odysseus speaks with Penelope and is almost revealed by Eurycleia.
Book Twenty	Odysseus and Telemachus prepare the hall for the impending battle. Penelope announces her challenge.
Book Twenty One	The Book of the bow.
Book Twenty Two	The slaughter in the Hall.
Book Twenty Three	Penelope and Odysseus are reunited.
Book Twenty Four	Odysseus is reunited with his father and a battle is fought between some of the Ithacans until the gods intervene and peace is restored.

1.2 The Oral tradition of Homer's *Odyssey*

In this section we will;

- *Understand what we do and do not know about 'Homer'*

- *Begin to consider the oral tradition and the textual transmission of the Odyssey*

- *To understand what the preliterate form of the Odyssey*

- *To consider some of the different theories surrounding the composition of the Odyssey*

The *Odyssey* as an oral work

The *Odyssey* therefore would differ in interpretation and quality depending on the skill of the poet and the freedom he was allowed to extemporise on the particular version of 'Homer' he was familiar with. Each performer would bring something different to the telling; a different tone, a re-ordering of some of the key events, lines added here or missed out there. Since there was no canonical, definitive version to work from the poet was much like a modern actor in a well-known and often acted play, who sought to perform and interpret the basic structure of the story in a new way for a particular audience. Perhaps some audiences would want longer scenes in some areas or shorter in others. In short then there was no one, standard *Odyssey*.

Therefore, we must not forget that although only one version of the original translation now remains, originally the *Odyssey* would have existed in many versions. Poets other than Homer would perform the *Odyssey* creating different performances and styles; with different interpretations of the same story.

The oral epic art form has largely been lost to the modern world, though remnants of an oral culture remain across many differing European countries and observations of Balkan poets guided the arguments of Homeric academics such as Milman and Lord. Attempts are made across the world to retell the *Odyssey* and the Iliad in the way it was originally recited. In fact, to get a flavour of the spoken, rather than written, quality of Homer, it is best to *hear* these poems rather than *read* them, wherever possible. One way to facilitate this is through listening to audio book or spoken word versions of the text; or simply to read the text aloud!

Hexameter verse

Described by Aristotle as *'the most solid and massive of metres',* Both the *Odyssey* and the *Iliad* are composed using Hexameter verse. Hexameter metre can vary from 12 to 17 syllables in each line, typically in 6 metrical units composed of dactyls and spondees. The hexameter verse structure allowed the oral poets to time their recital as well as combine set lines and phrases whilst also permitting some improvisation. The prime aim of hexameter verse was to aid the memorisation of lines as well as recite in tempo as the poet would often be accompanied by music.

These metrical units were either *dactyls* (a long syllable, followed by 2 short ones) or *spondees* (2 long syllables followed by a short).

A dactyl is a long syllable followed by two short. In English, this meter winds up sounding sing-songy. *Daktylos* is a word for a finger, which, with its 3 phalanges, is like a finger.

Theories of oral composition of the *Odyssey* and the *Iliad*.

The composition of the Iliad and the *Odyssey* has been the source of much debate for centuries. Where they created by one man Homer? Where they written or orally composed? When were they composed? Where were they composed? Whilst many of these questions remain unanswered and probably unanswerable, several theories have been composed;

Josephus (1st century AD). 'Homer did not leave his poems in writing....instead they were transmitted by memory and not unified until much later'.

Robert Wood (1769). 'Essay on the Original Genius of Homer' – Homer was as illiterate as Achilles and Odysseus.

Giambattista Vico (1668-1744) 'Homeric poems were the creation of the whole Greek people' (Composed over time by several poets).

F.A Wolf (1759-1824). 'If Homer was illiterate, how can the Odyssey and the Iliad be so long?'

It is clear then, that the identity of the individual or group that composed the *Odyssey* and the *Iliad* has long been a matter of discussion.

Milman Parry

Milman Parry (1928) concluded that Homer was a master of, and heir to, the tradition of oral epic poetry. Milman based his argument on the ornamental epithets used throughout both the *Iliad* and the *Odyssey*. These epithets are the high sounding labels used to describe individuals, places and objects such as;

- *'much enduring Odysseus'*

- *'rocky Ithaca'*

- *'hollow ships'*

Milman suggested that these epithets were used by poets who would use them to improvise lines of the epics in order to fulfil the requirements of hexameter verse. Homer, or the epic oral poets, improvised parts of the story, relying on stock phrases, lines and scenes as required rather than memorising the whole story. It is therefore probable that these improvisations resulted in a different telling of both the *Iliad* and *Odyssey* each time it was performed.

Homer and the Mycenaean context

In order to fully appreciate Homer's work it is important to understand something of the contextual history of the events described by Homer in his poems. The narrative events in both the *Iliad* and the *Odyssey* as well as the wider story of the events leading to and including the Trojan War are set in the semi historical period known today as the Mycenaean period of Ancient Greece.

Remember!

Do not assume that the poems of Homer are primarily historical documents: They are first and foremost literary works that post-date the Mycenaean Age considerably.

The Mycenaean period of Ancient Greece belongs to a chronological period spanning approximately from the 16th to the 12th centuries BC. It is named after the archaeological excavation of the Bronze Age period city of Mycenae, excavated from 1840 but most notably by Heinrich Schliemann during the 1870s. The site of Mycenae was one of several fortified palace sites discovered dating to the Mycenaean period across Greece.

It would be a mistake to assume that nothing in Homer is historical, since archaeological research has confirmed that there *is* indeed a fortification at Troy (now in modern Turkey, at a site close to a town called Hissarlik) that dates to the Mycenaean period. It has also been determined that the sea faring capabilities of the Bronze Age inhabitants of Greece were sufficient to undertake long distance voyages. It is therefore entirely possible that Mycenaean sea raiders or even a military expedition could have undertaken the long and costly expedition that would have been necessary to besiege and ultimately capture the site of 'Troy'; for reasons that have now been lost.

The archaeological discoveries of 'palace' based societies and economies have also confirmed that these palaces were central to the stability of Mycenaean civilisation. The palace sites and finds discovered at Mycenae, Tiryns and Pylos have confirmed the existence of sophisticated social, political and economic organisation. Large scale storage, skilled artisan work and even evidence of writing have been discovered at many of these archaeological sites.

Within Homer's works the duties of *xenia* (guest-friendship) and the heroic code are seen to be ultimately tied to this palace life and the stratified societies that they represent. As will be demonstrated, the themes of *xenia* and the heroic code feature strongly in the *Odyssey*, and understanding of these and other themes are crucial to developing an understanding of the poem.

Linear B language

By the twelfth century BC palace civilisations, including that of Mycenae and Pylos, collapsed. Why this occurred is uncertain. But as a result of this collapse many so called Mycenaean achievements were lost to the Greeks of the 8th century BC; one of these lost achievements was writing.

One of the most important finds of archaeological excavations from the Mycenaean world has been the discovery of clay tablets from sites including from Pylos (a site found on the West coast of the Peloponnese in Southern mainland Greece). Preserved by fire that destroyed parts of the palace at Pylos; these clay tablets were written in a script called 'Linear B'. This Linear B script remained a mystery to modern academics until 1952, when the amateur linguistic Michael Ventris deciphered Linear B and proved that the script was the ancestor of Classical Greek.

These tablets and the script they contain have proved invaluable in understanding the Mycenaean period, especially the administration, production and trade elements of society.

Homer probably did not know how to write; this is apparent in both the *Iliad* and the *Odyssey*. In these poems, nobody writes and there is no mention of written word. The skill of writing appeared to have become extinct along with the collapse of palace culture, and the beginning of the Greek Dark Age at the end of the twelfth century. For the inhabitants of the so called Greek 'dark age' from the 11th-8th century BC the ability to write appears to have lost its relevance.

1.3 Linguistic and stylistic techniques in Homer's *Odyssey*

In this section we will;

- *Explore and understand some key linguistic and stylistic techniques used in Homer's Odyssey*

- *Identify the distinctive features of Homeric style*

- *Practise finding and analysing some of these linguistic features present in the Odyssey*

- *Understand the narrative techniques, including flashback, retardation and episodes in the Odyssey*

Introduction

In this topic we will focus on some of the linguistic and stylistic techniques of Homer's *Odyssey*. In particular we will focus on using Books One to Three of the *Odyssey* in order to demonstrate some of these techniques. By introducing some linguistic and stylistic features of the *Odyssey* at this early stage in the guide we will establish a sound basis of understanding of oral composition.

Oral poetry

The poet or poets who constructed the Odyssey utilised many different stylistic and linguistic techniques.

These techniques not only add depth and complexity to the narrative of the Odyssey, but also were used to help the poet be able to time his performances and also to be able to remember the events and order of them. Remember after all that the Odyssey was a long poem and would have been performed probably over a period of several days. As such techniques such as repetition and regression of the story would help the audience to also keep track of the story.

> **Remember!**
>
> When reading Homer, it is important to remember that this epic poem was meant to be *heard*, not read.

When reading Homer, it is important to remember that this epic poem was meant to be *heard*, not read. Oral poetry is designed to be listened to. It is almost certain that Homer's poetry comes from a pre-literate period. With one bare exception, there is no mention of writing in either the *Iliad* of or the *Odyssey* and the techniques used in both poems strongly suggest that the poet (or poets) that created these stories was illiterate.

In the ancient world the idea of silent reading was somewhat unusual; typically someone reading a book would read out aloud as they read. When considering the epic poetry of Homer, it is important to bear in mind that the poet would recite and the audience would listen.

Features of Oral poetry

Oral poetry differs from written poetry in several ways.

Below are two key features of oral poetry;

- *Repetition*

- *Digression or Retardation of the plot*

What is Repetition?

One of the most apparent techniques of oral poetry is the use of repetition.

Prime examples of kinds of repetition used by Homer include;

- Words, phrases and sentences are commonly repeated in the *Odyssey* such as 'noble Odysseus', 'insolent Suitors' or 'He called to his men and they obeyed'.

- At the level of the scene and scenes of action certain stock phrases are repeated. Typically this can be seen in scenes of battle or feasting, but can also be seen in the lies told by Odysseus.

- Homer also uses pairs of characters to play out a particular scenario. For example, Telemachus and Athena in book 1 and the two leading faithful servants at Ithaca; Philoetius and Eumaeus in Book Twenty One to provide two examples out of many.

Repetition is of vital importance to the oral poet. Repetition helps to fix the poem in mind of the performer, and maintains the flow and rhythm of the poem.

Task: Examples of Repetition in Books One to Three

Go through the *Odyssey* Books One to Three.

Identify at least three examples of repetition in these books.

This is important as you can use these as examples of this feature of oral poetry in the exams.

What is Retardation of the plot?

Retardation of the plot, also called a *digression or elaboration*, is another technique used by Homer in the *Odyssey*. This second feature allows the oral poet to develop the interest of the narrative into a related anecdote, but still leaves room to return to the main story and plot. This digression is a common feature of epic and is used by Homer to elaborate his descriptions of people and places.

Retardation of the plot is a strong feature of interaction between characters in the *Odyssey*. When characters they tell each other stories in the *Odyssey* they often digress. These digressions are sometimes allowed to go on at some length, but the main thread of the narrative is always returned to by the use of signals such as *'as I was saying earlier...'*.

Retardation of the plot is now often described as *'ring composition'*. Ring composition is so called because the narrative returns to where it left off in a circular fashion.

Ring composition is a controlling feature of the oral poet that ensures that, despite the retardations, the main storyline still takes precedence and the direction of that is kept moving to its end.

Task: Retardation of the plot in Books One to Three

Go through the *Odyssey* Books 1-3.

Identify at least two examples of repetition in these books.

This is important as you can use these as examples of this feature of oral poetry in the exams.

Examples of repetition in the *Odyssey*

The first, most noticeably non-modern feature of the *Odyssey* (and a direct result of its oral composition and performance, as has already been discussed) is the so-called *'formulae'* of repeated words and phrases.

'Formulae' function much as do repeated phrases, words and choruses in song and poetry today. They are a means of fitting the words and general plot to the strict demands of the metre and as a handle for the poet when reciting the works from memory.

Take note!

Some of the 'formulae' you may have noted in the first few books of the *Odyssey* include:

- *'bright-eyed' goddess (applied to Athena)*

- *'fresh and rosy-fingered' (applied to the Dawn)*

- *'courteous Telemachus'*

Retardation in Books One to Three

There are two short examples of ring composition in the first three books of the *Odyssey*. There are longer and more noticeable examples to come.

Some good examples of Ring composition include;

- Book One, lines 113-119

- Book Two, lines 270-272 and 278-280

In the first example, Telemachus catches sight of Athena, and the digression involves Telemachus revealing his thoughts, feelings and desires for his father's *'nostos'* or homecoming.

In the second of these examples, the goddess Athena is disguised as Mentor. Athena converses with Telemachus about the great qualities of Odysseus the hero, these qualities are traits which Telemachus himself has inherited.

These digressions establish Telemachus' status as the true son of Penelope and Odysseus, a hero in waiting, and come before the main thrust of Athena's argument; that Telemachus should seek news of his father.

Task: Language and style in Homer

Write a response to the following question;

How far do you agree that the Homer's use of retardation of the plot and repetition help to enrich the story of Odysseus?

1.4 Shaping meaning: The Homeric Simile

In this section we will;

- *Explore and understand some key linguistic and stylistic techniques used in Homer's Odyssey*

- *Familiarise ourselves with the distinctive features of Homeric similes*

- *Identify the distinctive features of Homeric style.*

- *Practise finding and analysing some of these linguistic features present in the Odyssey*

Introduction

In this topic we focus on some of the other linguistic and stylistic techniques of Homer's *Odyssey*.

In particular we will focus on using Books One to Three of the *Odyssey* in order to demonstrate some of these techniques. By introducing some linguistic and stylistic features of the *Odyssey* at this early stage in the guide we will establish a sound basis of understanding of oral composition.

The Homeric Simile

Below is a good example of the Homeric simile, our first introduction to another of Homer's literary techniques, the *simile;*

"The Suitors were scared out of their senses. They scattered through the hall like a herd of cattle that a darting gadfly had attacked and stampeded, in the spring-time when the long days come in".

Book XXII.300-302

> ### *Simile*
>
> A *simile* is a common literary technique that is a comparison of one item with another with which it intentionally similar. Generally speaking if something is like something else then this is a simile. So for example in Homer's *Odyssey* Menelaus likens Odysseus to a lion and the suitors to startled deer. Another example is to compare the love of a character to a beautiful flower such as a rose.

The difference between a metaphor and a simile.

A metaphor is a figure of speech that compares a subject to another which is otherwise unrelated. Comparing your life to a journey is a metaphor, or like Shakespeare in his play 'As you like it';

"All the world is a stage,

And all the men and women merely players;

They have their exits and their entrances"

A simile is *not* the same as a metaphor; it is introduced by a comparison word such as 'like' or 'as' or even 'just as'. The comparison is made but, unlike a metaphor the items of comparison are not identified with each other. Homeric similes are typically determined and real-life: Homer is particularly fond of using animals or the natural world as to what is going on in the poem. Homer compares or else references the type of experiences that would have been known to Greeks of his time. So, ships and sailing feature, as do activities such as cooking and hunting. They can at times even be humorous.

Task: Analysing a Homeric simile

Read the following excerpt and the answer the questions below;

"Auburn haired Menelaus was hot with indignation. 'How disgraceful! He cried. 'So the cowards want to creep into the brave man's bed? It's just as if a deer had put her two little unweaned fawns to sleep in a mighty lion's den and gone to range the high ridges and grassy dales for pasture. Back comes the lion to his lair, and the fawns meet a grisly fate – as will the Suitors at Odysseus' hand."

Homer's *Odyssey* Book IV. 331-340

Ensure that you are able to write a brief response to the following questions;

- What is the subject of the simile in this passage?

- What do you think the effect of this simile is here?

- How effective do you think it is in conveying an image to the audience?

Menelaus' simile

The similes used by Homer are typically extensions of the previous sentence. In the above example, the simile serves to contrast between the bravery of Odysseus against the cowardly nature of the Suitors. The animal comparison between the predator; the lion, and the prey; the deer, is particularly apt. Odysseus is destined to hunt down the Suitors on his return to Ithaca and Menelaus assumes *will* happen and will take just revenge for their behaviour; as is appropriate for a Homeric hero to do.

Task: Identifying Homeric Similes.

Explore the books of the *Odyssey* that you have read so far.

Try to find at least three good examples of Homeric similes.

For each simile consider;

- What is the nature of the comparison?

- What do you think the effect of this simile is?

Other language and stylistic techniques in Homer's *Odyssey*

The following is a list of literary methods that we can identify in Homer's *Odyssey*;

- *Allusion*

- *Analepsis*

- *Apotheosis*

- *Deus ex Machina*

- *Epithet*

- *Intertextuality*

- *Metaphor*

- *Metonym*

- *Personification*

- *Prolepsis*

- *Symbol*

Allusion - An *allusion* is a direct or indirect reference to other literary texts. In Virgil for example we can most easily identify allusions to the works of Homer, whilst in the *Odyssey* we encounter allusions drawn from the *Iliad*.

Analepsis - *Analepsis* is a form of 'flashback'; a digression by the poet when they refer to events that have occurred previously. *Analepsis* can be either brief or extended. For example in book two of the *Odyssey* Nestor tells of his trip back from Troy.

Apotheosis - *Apotheosis* is a literary device by which a character is transformed or elevated to a god-like status. At the end of Euripides' *Medea* for example Medea flies away in a chariot drawn by dragons, a clear transformation from her state at the beginning of the tragedy.

Deus ex Machina - A literary device used by poets, playwrights and authors to bring about a resolution of a conflict or situation through the deployment of the actions of a god, character or action that may seem otherwise unrelated to the story.

Epithet – An *epithet* is a name bestowed upon a character which identifies a defining characteristic. For example in Homer's Odyssey for example Odysseus is often referred to as 'resourceful' or 'cunning'.

Intertextuality - Often a writer or poet will make reference to the works of another writer or poet. For example it is often stated that Virgil makes direct or indirect references to the works of Homer.

Metaphor – A common literary device that is present in everyday usage by us all. A metaphor is a merging of two different elements or ideas. For example to say *'My head is spinning'* is a metaphor. Likewise Shakespeare famously used the metaphor *'All the world's a stage…'* in his play *As you like it.*

Metonym - A Metonym is the use of a part in order to represent the whole; the use of one item to stand for another for which it has been associated. For example in common usage the news channels refer to the UK government as 'Westminster'. Another example is the presentation of a clock in film to represent time passing. A final example of a Metonym is to refer to the police as the long arm of the law.

Personification – Personification is when an inhuman object is given human characteristics.

Prolepsis - *Prolepsis* is a 'fast-forward'; a digression by the poet or writer when they refer to events that have occurred previously. Like *analepsis* , *prolepsis* can be either brief or extended.

Symbol - A device used by writers and poets to substitute one thing for another. These symbols replace a word with an item associated with this word. So for example a Dove is commonly used as a symbol for peace. Red is a colour we commonly associate with danger and a snake is sometimes used as a symbol for temptation.

Task: Understanding key literary and linguistic devices

Below are some examples of text.

Identify the techniques being used.

So for example – *'My love is a rose'* is a metaphor.

a) Messapus tamer of horses
b) The wine dark sea
c) The moon was a ghostly ship tossed about on cloudy seas
d) Man killing Hector

A passage from Virgil's *Aeneid;*

"At that moment I seemed to see the whole of Ilium settling into the flames and Neptune's Troy toppling over from its foundations like as ancient ash tree high in the mountains which farmers have hacked with blow upon blow of their double axes, labouring to fell it..."

Virgil *Aeneid* II.625-628.

Now for a longer passage from the *Aeneid*, with multiple techniques.

"Just as Mars, spattered with blood, charges along the banks of the icy river Hebrus, clashing sword on shield and giving full rein to his furious horses as he stirs up war, they fly across the open plain before the winds of the south and west, til Thrace roars to its furthest reaches with the drumming of their hooves as his escort gallops all round him, Rage, Treachery and the dark faces of Fear – just so did bold Turnus lash his horses through the thick of battle til they smoked with sweat, and as he trampled the pitiable bodies of his dead enemies , the flying hooves scattered a dew of blood and churned the gore into the sand."

Virgil *Aeneid* XII.333-340.

1.5 The Homeric Hero

In this section we will;

- *To investigate the similarities and differences between our concept of 'heroes' and those portrayed by Homer*

- *To understand the concepts of Honour (timé) and Reputation (kleos)*

Introduction to *time and kleos*

Two cultural concepts require some explanation before proceeding into the *Odyssey* proper.

Odysseus is a hero, and as such is expected to act in particular ways. In order to fit the mould of a hero; Odysseus needs to be brave, resourceful and at times violent. In particular the Ancient Greeks used two conceptual terms which were of specific concern to the Greek heroes. This section will examine these concepts; Honour *(timé)* and Reputation *(kleos)*.

Task: Identifying 'Heroic' traits

Think about the following well known characters from literature and from films - write a list of the traits and powers that make this character 'heroic'.

- James Bond
- Harry Potter
- Wonder Woman
- Your own favourite "hero"

What is a Hero?

The Hero can take many forms; from Superman or Spiderman with their superpowers to Bilbo Baggins from Tolkien's *The Hobbit* – In himself Bilbo has no special superpowers but his struggle and determination sees him through to success in the end.

Still other kinds of hero can be identified from real life; such as those that face dangerous illnesses with courage, raise money for charities or someone who rescues people from burning buildings.

Heroes can take many shapes and forms, but they do share many characteristics; they are brave, they may work as a force for good, they can be selfish or selfless and they more often as not win through in the end and triumph over the challenges that they are faced with.

The ancient Greek concept of the Hero: *timé* and *kleos*

The *Iliad*, more so than the *Odyssey*, the subject matter deals with what it is to be one of the hero class, such as an Achilles or an Agamemnon. It centred on achieving the value *timé* (honour or esteem).

Being a hero, or warrior, was a distinctly elitist pursuit, since only such men in the Homeric world have the nobility of mind to fight in battle (and the wealth to do so). This was paralleled to an extent in the Classical period, an individual's wealth determined their ability to fight, with the richest serving as cavalry, the middle classes serving as heavy armoured infantry (hoplites) and the poorer serving as light armed skirmishers, or excluded from fighting entirely.

Key terms:

timé – The pursuit of honour and esteem.

kleos – Good reputation.

An example of *timé from the Iliad*

"But powerful Diomedes froze him with a glance:

"Not a word of retreat. You'll never persuade me.

It's not my nature to shrink from battle, cringe in fear

With the fighting strength still steady in my chest.

I shrink from mounting our chariot – no retreat-

On foot as I am, I'll meet them man to man.

Athena would never let me flinch."

Iliad Book V, 278 – 284 (translated by R.Fagles).

Martial valour was a way for the elite of the Homeric world to ensure their *timé*, and thus to secure their *kleos* (good reputation: the things, good and bad, that people say about you) on the battlefield.

Not only was warfare a desirable pursuit of the elite, it was also their duty to fight when called upon in order to protect the palace and outlying territories which they ruled. A refusal to fight in these circumstances was a rejection of obligation. It was expected that a king or war leader should act in a heroic way, in return for which he received the loyalty of his subordinates and the dues from them necessary for his status as their leader. The world of Homer then was distinctly feudal in nature.

Remember!

For Homer, the key to being a hero was the desire for *timé* and the concern for their future *kleos*.

An example of *kleos* from the *Iliad*

"Hector loosing a savage cry and flaring on like fire,

Like the God of fire, the blaze that never dies.

And the cry pierced Menelaus, deeply torn now

as he probed his own great heart: "What can I do?

If I leave this splendid gear and desert Patroclus-

fell here fighting, all to redeem my honour-

Won't any comrade curse me, seeing me break away?

But if I should take on Hector and Hector's Trojans

alone, in single combat – trying to save my pride –

won't they encircle me, one against so many?"

Iliad XVII, 100-107 (translated by R.Fagles).

Remember!

Kleos

kleos is renown. *Kleos* can also refer to praise poetry and this renown is most especially valued, as it is these deeds that can result in fame beyond death. Achilles for example is a Greek hero that sought (and found) immortality, due to his *kleos*.

In the example above Menelaus is concerned how it will look if he tries to protect the corpse of Patroclus against all odds or instead retreat and save himself to fight another day. In the event he makes a sensible decision and calls others to help him making demands of their own *kleos* (whilst maintaining his own good standing).

Heroes in the world of Homer value their honour and consequently their reputation or 'good name' more than any other concern. Through winning battles, fighting honourably; especially in single-combat and hopefully, victory ensures this. However, the negative aspects of *timé* and *kleos* lay in the ever-present reality of an early and untimely death in battle. This is what Achilles chooses when he sails to Troy, and his death ensures that his name will be preserved for eternity. This was the price paid by the hero in return for the only thing considered to be of any worth in the world of Homer.

Task: Identifying examples of timé and kleos in the Odyssey

Having read the Odyssey it will be useful to consolidate your understanding of the concepts of time and kleos by identifying two examples of each from across the Odyssey.

These examples can come from any character and from any point of the Odyssey.

Part Two: The *Telemachy*

Part Two: The *Telemachy*

2.1 Xenia in the *Odyssey*

2.2 Book One: Athena inspires Telemachus

2.3 Book Two: The Ithacan debate: style and realism

2.4 Book Three: Nestor

2.5 Book Four: Menelaus and story telling

The *Telemachy*

Since they are entirely about Telemachus' own journey to establish his own authority and to grow into his role as future king; the first four books of the *Odyssey* are sometimes referred to as the '*Telemachy*'. In the time that has passed since the end of the Trojan War and '*Nostos*', or the homecoming of Odysseus, Telemachus has grown up to become a young man, and he has grown up in a very difficult situation. Odysseus' long absence is beginning to hurt; ambitious nobles from Ithaca and the surrounding lands are eager to seize hold of Odysseus' wife and the wealth and authority that would come with such a marriage.

In the early books of the *Odyssey*, Telemachus must learn how to be a man and take responsibility for his mother, his home and Ithaca. In doing so, Telemachus will then become a vital ally of Odysseus in the climatic events of the final books of the *Odyssey*.

The journey to Pylos and then Sparta by Telemachus provides a counter-point to the '*Odyssey*', the journeys of Odysseus himself. Telemachus is recognised as the son of Odysseus by the veterans of Troy, Nestor and Menelaus, and show that Telemachus is a worthy son to his father. Telemachus also sees the 'proper relationship of son to father at the palace of Pylos. Telemachus is also informed of the danger his father (and also to himself) should his mother determine to marry one of the Suitors in the tale of the murder of Agamemnon the lover of his own wife Clytemnestra, Aegisthus.

2.1 *Xenia* in the *Odyssey*

This section will help you to;

- *Read Book One of the Odyssey*

- *Begin to understand the concept of xenia and its use in the Odyssey*

- *Consider other examples of positive and negative xenia in the Odyssey*

Introduction

This section will help you to understand the role of *xenia* in the *Odyssey*. *Xenia* – or 'guest friendship' is a crucial part of the Odyssey and lay at the crux of the whole of Homer's epic poem. It is through positive practice of *xenia* that we see Telemachus transform from an adolescent into a man through his travels to Pylos and Sparta. It is through positive practice of *xenia* that Odysseus is transported by the Phaeacians back to Ithaca – at some cost to themselves.

Likewise it is the abuse of *xenia* that we see the trials and tribulations of Odysseus – it is the Suitors' abuse of *xenia* that sees them loitering around the absent Odysseus' palace and results in their grisly demise.

Xenia

Xenia, or guest friendship, is an important cultural and social value in the *Odyssey* and one that is vital to understand in order to understand fully the events of the *Odyssey*.

The Greek word *xenia* has no direct translation into English. It is commonly rendered as 'hospitality' or 'guest-friendship', but its significance runs deeper than either definition given above. The practice of *xenia* was a code of conduct for dealing with strangers and visitors and was expected in the Greek world.

This ritualised behaviour ensured that both the visitor and the host would be protected and honoured by the meeting. The good practice of *xenia* was an important part of the Ancient Greek moral code that Homer, and his audience, would take for granted. In the

Classical Greek period (approximately 600-300BC) the sacrosanct nature of Heralds operating between often hostile cities was derived in a large part from the practice of *xenia*.

Broadly speaking, the practice of *xenia* ritualised the duties and obligations placed upon both a guest and a host. The guest, either an expected guest or as Odysseus most often is, unexpected, was required to behave in a polite and respectful way to his host and where possible, to give a ceremonial gift of some expense, such as an item of weaponry, or a decorative item such as a plate, vase or platter.

In return it was the host's responsibility, as divinely ordained by Zeus, the patron deity of guests and thus of *xenia*, to offer shelter, food, drink and hospitality to any such strangers (or known guests) who might arrive on his doorstep.

The role of *xenia* in the *Odyssey*

> **Xenia**
>
> *'Guest friendship' is a bond of trust that imitates kinship and often ritualised, creates obligations between individuals belonging to different social units.*

As mentioned above, without the use or rather the misuse of *xenia* in the *Odyssey*, Homer would not have a story to tell. From the outset we see the abuse of *xenia* at Ithaca; the Suitors have taken advantage of Odysseus' absence to make a nuisance of themselves and are making both Telemachus and Penelope's lives a nightmare. It is the demonstration of the good practice of *xenia* by Nestor and Menelaus which shows Telemachus just how badly the Suitors are acting.

Likewise, by preventing the escape of Odysseus from her island, Calypso abuses the right of a guest to leave whenever they desire; despite the beauty and allure of her home. In short then, without the cultural practise of *xenia*, the *Odyssey* would not be the same poem.

Guest Friendship in Book One

The concept of Guest Friendship (*xenia*) pervades the *Odyssey* and is of paramount importance to the hero Odysseus, as well as his son Telemachus. It is the abuse of his guests that drives Telemachus to seek news of his Father and starts in motion the *Odyssey*.

In Book 1 we see both the best and worst of *xenia* – the practice of excellent *xenia* by Telemachus to the disguised Athena on the one hand, and the abuse of the laws of hospitality by the Suitors on the other.

The custom and entrenched social value of *xenia* was so important in which the world outside of one's immediate doorstep was often one fraught with danger and the unknown, and so a fellow Greek-speaker who was far from his home deserved the help and hospitality that any in his position would need. Typically, we see *xenia* in the *Odyssey* between members of the aristocratic class who honour one another for being fellow aristocrats, but it is certainly a marker of civilisation, of civilized values and of humanity in the *Odyssey*, as shall become apparent later.

Xenia in Book Three and Four

In Book Three we see perhaps the most idealised example of *xenia*; Nestor and his sons invite Telemachus and the disguised Athena to share their meal and prayers before questioning them as to their names and the purpose of their visit. After an exchange of information and advice, Nestor bids his guest farewell and sees Telemachus off in a borrowed chariot filled with gifts and piloted by his son.

Upon reaching Sparta, we see another good example of positive *xenia*; after rebuking his squire for hesitating to offer his hospitality, Menelaus invites Telemachus and the son of Nestor to eat and to wash. Once again, when it is time for Telemachus to leave, Menelaus does not detain him but instead hastens him on accompanied by gifts.

In direct contrast to this idealised examples of xenia, Book Four sees the Suitors plotting to murder Telemachus on his journey back to Ithaca.

Task: *Xenia* in Book One

Read Book One of the *Odyssey* from line 100 to the end of the Book.

Complete the following table, recording examples of both positive and negative *xenia* in Book One.

Positive examples of *xenia* in Book One	Negative examples of *xenia* in Book Two

Reading about *xenia*

Read the following passages of Homer's *Odyssey*;

- Book 3.30-80

- Book 3.470-488

- Book 4.20-75

- Book 4.650-672

These are examples of the practice of *xenia* in the early part of the Odyssey. We recommend that as many examples of *xenia* should be examined as possible.

2.2 Book One: Athena inspires Telemachus

In this section we will;

- *Explore and understand the content and style of Book One of the Odyssey*

- *Explore the ways in which Homer uses language to engage the audience*

- *Understand the role and purposes of the proem*

- *Introduce some of the leading characters in the Odyssey*

- *Consider why Odysseus is absent in the early part of the Odyssey*

- *Examine the role of Telemachus in the early part of the Odyssey*

- *Begin to consider some of the stylistic techniques used by Homer*

- *Begin to consider some of the linguistic techniques used by Homer*

Book I of the *Odyssey*

This section will help you to understand the first book of the *Odyssey*. Here Homer introduces the story of Odysseus and introduces some of the main characters of his epic poem. One noticeable absence from Book One is Odysseus himself and we begin to consider why Odysseus is absent from the events unfolding in Books One through Four.

> ***Task: Comprehending Book One***
>
> *Read Book One of the Odyssey*
>
> *Once you have, write brief responses to the following questions;*
>
> - *How has Homer chosen to start his work?*
> - *What has Homer focussed on in Book One?*
> - *What has Homer left out in Book One?*

Book One: Synopsis

In Book One of the *Odyssey*, Homer invokes a Muse to tell through his voice the story of Odysseus, a Greek hero who fought at Troy and now after an absence of twenty years is to conclude his journey home. Homer tells us that Odysseus is trapped on an island ruled by a Godlike Nymph named Calypso. All of his men are dead, the last of them killed by the Gods as punishment for eating the cattle of the Sun god Hyperion (also called Helios).

Here though Homer shifts the focus of the story away from the hero Odysseus and instead to a council of Gods who now decree that Odysseus be allowed to return to his home on the island of Ithaca. It is decided that Hermes will travel to Calypso and order her to release Odysseus whilst Athena will travel to Ithaca to visit Telemachus, the son of Odysseus.

Homer then shifts the scene again, to Ithaca itself, where Odysseus is considered to be dead. His home and property are being consumed by an army of young men, all eager to marry Odysseus' wife Penelope and take over as king of Ithaca themselves. Penelope however refuses to choose a suitor and her son Telemachus watches the Suitors in impotent anger as they consume his father's property and his inheritance.

It is to Telemachus that the Goddess Athena descends from Mount Olympus. In disguise as a Taphian ship captain named Mentes, Athena visits Telemachus and urges the young man to become more assertive in the face of the Suitors and to seek out news of Odysseus, whom Athena declares, is finally on his way home. Athena suggests that Telemachus travel to Pylos and Sparta to visit his father's companions in arms Nestor and Menelaus and learn from them what they can tell him of the fate of his father.

Telemachus suspects that he has been visited by a god and therefore begins to address the suitors more sternly and also determines to obey the instruction to travel to Pylos and Sparta and seek out news of his long lost father.

The Structure of Book One

Book One of the *Odyssey* can most easily be divided into five sections;

- The *Proem* (lines 1-11)

- Homer elaborates on the *Proem* (lines 12-21)

- The Gods debate the fate of Odysseus (lines 22-96)

- Telemachus and Athena (lines 113-320)

- Telemachus, Penelope and the Suitors (lines 321-444)

Characters in Book One

The following characters are present in Book One of the Odyssey;

- *Zeus*

- *Athena*

- *Telemachus*

- *Athena disguised as Mentes*

- *Phemius the bard*

- *Penelope*

- *Antinous, a leading suitor*

- *Eurymachus, a leading suitor*

- *Eurycleia, a loyal household slave*

The *Proem (lines 1-11)*

These first lines of the *Odyssey* are called the 'proem', which comes from the Greek word *'proemium'*, which simply means the introduction.

The first eleven lines of the *Odyssey* are noticeably different from the rest of the poem. Unlike the rest of the poem, these initial lines take the form of a prayer or invocation to the Muse.

At the start of epic, Homer calls upon the Goddess or Muse. Homer either believes or adopts the stance that the poem couldn't be composed without divine inspiration. This is an Invocation.

> **Key term:**
>
> **Invocation:**
> At the start of epic, Homer calls upon the Goddess or Muse. Homer either believes or adopts the stance that the poem couldn't be composed without divine inspiration.

The Muses were the Ancient Greek goddesses of the Arts, which poets and other artists called upon to help them craft their poems, sculptures and plays. As the daughters of Zeus, the Muses could also punish those who attempted to create artistic products without first offering prayers or seeking the assistance of the Muse. Incidentally, the word 'Museum' comes from the name of a holy site that was dedicated to the Muses.

As well invoking the assistance of the Muse; the *proem* sets the scene for the rest of the *Odyssey*, without giving too much of the story away to the audience. A modern equivalent to the proem could be a film trailer that shows just enough of the film to appeal to potential audiences, without giving away the plot or the spectacle.

The *proem* contains no mention of Telemachus, Odysseus' son, who is the key character of the first three books of the *Odyssey*. Rather, the function of the *proem* is to establish the moral tone for the *Odyssey*. The *proem* clearly states that Odysseus' crew will die and moreover, that they fully deserved their deaths. This theme of deserved punishment continues throughout the *Odyssey* and is elaborated on in Book One with regards to the Suitors.

Homer's interjection *(lines 12-21)*

Having invoked the Muse to tell the story of Odysseus, Homer now provides a brief section of contextual information. The Trojan War has ended and Troy is destroyed. All the surviving Greeks have returned home, with one exception; Odysseus. Odysseus is a prisoner of the Nymph Calypso who keeps him in the hope that he will marry her. Now however all the Gods except Poseidon desire that Odysseus should return to Ithaca, his home and his family.

The Gods debate the fate of Odysseus *(lines 22-96)*

Homer chooses to begin the *Odyssey* with a meeting of the gods on Olympus. Poseidon is absent in Ethiopia and Athena uses the opportunity offered to petition Zeus that now is the time for Odysseus to return home.

Zeus is sympathetic to Athena's appeal. He says he has been giving thought to Odysseus' misfortune and does not desire Odysseus to suffer the same fate as Agamemnon, who arrived home only to be murdered by Aegisthus, the lover of his wife Clytemnestra.

In lines 34-37 Homer has Zeus declare that mortals too often blame the gods for their own misfortune. This he says is not the case. Rather it is mortals themselves who bring about their own disasters even when the gods warn them not to. Aegisthus is a prime example of this. Hermes was sent to warn him not to take Clytemnestra as his lover and not to murder Agamemnon. Aegisthus was warned but killed Agamemnon anyway and was slain by Agamemnon's son Orestes in return.

Athena responds declaring that she has no sympathy for Aegisthus, but she does for Odysseus. Zeus agrees but now provides us with a little more information. Poseidon is angry with Odysseus because he blinded his son, the Cyclops Polyphemus (lines 70-80). Athena is used to end this divine debate with a plan. She will go to Ithaca to inspire Telemachus, whilst Hermes should be sent to Calypso to order her to free Odysseus.

Just as Homer begins the *Odyssey* starts with the prayer to the Muse in the *proem*, Homer continues with the divine by beginning the dialogue of the *Odyssey* with immortal rather than mortal characters. This 'council of the gods' is important as it reminds the audience that Odysseus has divine support and that it is his destiny to return home.

Telemachus and Athena (lines 113-320)

Having introduced the overall plot and set the scene, Homer now directs our attention to the bulk of the action in Book One. He does not start his poem at the beginning of the story, rather he begins the Odyssey in *media res*. Athena takes on a human disguise and visits Telemachus at his home on Ithaca.

Athena takes on the form of Mentes, a Taphian ship captain and enters the palace. Here we see Homer portray the wealth and opulence of Odysseus' home and also how it is being treated by the suitors in lines 108-112 the suitors are butchering livestock and taking their leisure at the expense of the absent hero. In the midst of the suitors sits Telemachus in misery. He does not like what the suitors are doing, but has no idea what to do about it and the suitors know this.

On seeing Athena disguised as Mentes, Telemachus at once welcomes this stranger and offers perfect xenia, which contrasts strongly with the deeds and actions of his other, less welcome visitors. Telemachus makes his new guest welcome, placing them in a chair as far away as possible from the suitors and feeding Mentes before enquiring as to the reason for his visit.

As the bard Phemius begins his song Telemachus uses the cover of the music to ask questions of Mentes. He asks who he is and where he is from. Athena, disguised as the Taphian ship captain Mentes responds and adds that he has come because he has heard rumour that his old friend Odysseus has returned (lines 195-200). Athena continues with a prophecy for Telemachus, that Odysseus will soon return.

The conversation now switches to discussing the suitors. In lines 222-229 Athena, disguised as Mentes inquires of Telemachus about the suitors. Telemachus replies that the suitors are unwelcome guests (lines 230-251) and fears that they will kill him or drive him out of his home. Telemachus doubts that Odysseus will return. He has been gone so long he *must* be dead.

> **Key term:**
>
> *In medias res:*
>
> *Into the middle of things, the epic story begins in the middle of things and reveals the past with narratives and flashbacks.*

Athena seeks to inspire Telemachus, who even doubts that he is the son of Odysseus, so powerless he feels to act. In lines 290-300, Athena reminds Telemachus of Orestes, the son of Agamemnon who avenged his father and seeks to inspire a bit of backbone into the young prince;

'You are no longer a child: you must put childish thoughts away...'

The appeal is supported with some advice. Telemachus should seek out news of Odysseus. He should travel to visit Nestor at Pylos and Menelaus at Sparta; Odysseus' old comrades at arms during the Trojan War and learn from them any news they can give him of his father.

The conversation between Telemachus and Athena disguised as Mentes is brought to an end with more examples of the good practice of xenia. Telemachus offers his guest a gift and does not seek to detain Mentes longer than he desires. For her part, Athena as Mentes refuses to take the gift now but asks that Telemachus keep it safe. Mentes departs and Telemachus rapidly comes to believe that he has been visited by a god.

Task: Exploring the banquet scene in Book One

Read Book One of the Odyssey lines 112-157

- *What kinds of language does Homer use to describe the wealth and splendour of the palace in these lines?*
- *How effectively does Homer contrast the actions of Telemachus and the actions of the suitors in these lines?*

Telemachus, Penelope and the Suitors (lines 321-444)

The final episode of Book One now commences with the arrival of Penelope. She has heard Phemius performing his sad song about the disasters inflicted upon the returning Greek heroes from Troy.

Penelope urges Phemius to sing about something else but Telemachus confronts his mother and orders her out of the feast hall and to go to bed. He clearly announces that he 'is master in this house' (line 359). Penelope is surprised by Telemachus forcefulness and retires.

The Suitors now begin to make their presence felt. Some raise catcalls and state that they should join Penelope in bed and once again Telemachus surprises them. He challenges them and urges that they be more respectful; if they do not he will pray to Zeus that he be allowed to destroy them as they are destroying his father's property (line378-380)

Two suitors rise to this challenge; Antinous and Eurymachus. The issue of kingship in Ithaca; Antinous prays it will never be Telemachus, whilst Eurymachus is more interested in Telemachus' recently departed guest. Who was he?

**Key term:
Polyphonic**

Literally means 'many voiced'.

The term Polyphonic means that there are many speakers in this part of the poem.

Telemachus now begins to demonstrate more emphatically that he is his father's son. He has confronted the suitors and challenged their views of him. He now deceives them. Telemachus strongly suspects that he has been visited by a god. But he does not reveal this. Likewise, he now strongly suspects that Odysseus is on his way home, yet he declares that Odysseus must be dead. Telemachus then is now taking steps to become his father's son; a hero in his own right by demonstrating bravery and willpower in confronting the suitors and also by deliberately misleading the suitors as to his places and thoughts on the fate of Odysseus.

The first book of the Odyssey now ends with bedtime. Telemachus retires to his bedroom, his head full of schemes. His attendant is also introduced briefly. Eurycleia, a loyal house slave and a motherly figure for Telemachus ensures that he reaches his bed chamber.

The absence of Odysseus in Book One

As mentioned above, one individual is notable by his absence in Book One. Odysseus has no direct role to play at this point. This is an intentional device used by Homer. By telling the story of Odysseus' long journey home from the Trojan War non-chronologically, Homer allows the audience to understand the impact of Odysseus' absence from Ithaca and to further reinforce the influence of Odysseus' return in the final half of the *Odyssey*.

Instead of starting with Odysseus departing from Troy after the end of the Trojan War, and then telling all the events that befall him before finally arriving back home again, and then what happened on Ithaca once he did arrive back, the audience are plunged into the middle of the action many years into Odysseus' long absence from home.

Homer has several main purposes in beginning the *Odyssey* in this way;

- By beginning with the effects of Odysseus' absence it is possible to see the problems inflicted on his family and people in Ithaca, the *Odyssey* portrays a situation that can only be solved by the arrival of the hero.

- By beginning the narrative in this way, Homer also allows Telemachus to develop from a boy into a son worthy of his heroic father.

- By beginning the narrative this way, Homer also establishes the role of the goddess Athena as the divine protector of Odysseus and his family.

Stylistic techniques used by Homer in Book One

In Book One of the *Odyssey* a great deal happens in a short space of time. The audience is introduced to the story, the will of the gods and sees the situation that awaits Odysseus at home when he finally reaches it. The action shifts from an appeal to the Muse, to the home of the Gods on Olympus and finally to the palace of Odysseus on Ithaca.

Homer also ensures that the audience are exposed to a number of the most important characters in the poem; Telemachus, Athena, Penelope as well as several of the suitors. Other minor characters make their presence known; even without saying a word such as Phremius and Eurycleia.

Homer also raises the parallel myth of Agamemnon, his murder by Aegisthus and the subsequent vengeance of Orestes in Book One. This parallel myth is important as it identifies for the audience a possible fate for Odysseus should Penelope decide to give up on the safe return of Odysseus and select a new husband. For Telemachus then would be the choice of reprising the role of Orestes or choosing permanent exile.

> **Task: Exploring the portrayal of characters in Book One**
>
> - *What kinds of language does Homer use to describe the character and personality of Penelope and the Suitors in Book One?*
> - *How convincingly does Homer portray the troubles confronting Telemachus in Book One?*
> - *Why do you think Homer chooses to introduce characters such as Phemius and Eurycleia in Book One?*

Linguistic techniques used by Homer in Book One

In Book One Homer begins a technique that he uses more fully in Book Two. Book One is a *polyphonic* part of the poem; with many speakers all having their say.

Homer includes a brief simile in Book One. In lines 305-308 Telemachus likens the advice provided by the disguised Athena to that given *'like a father to his son'*. This simile is especially appropriate for Book One, because Telemachus is not only lacking a father figure at home, he is also seeking information about the fate of his father and this good advice will enable Telemachus to find himself and prepare to assist his father once he inevitably returns.

Another linguistic technique evident in Book One is the brief digression on the background of the household slave Eurycleia in lines 428-436. This brief backstory for Eurycleia helps to give emphasis and foreshadowing of her future role in the Odyssey once Odysseus finally achieves his *Nostos*; or homecoming.

2.3 Book Two: The Ithacan debate: style and realism

In this section we will;

- *Explore and understand the content and style of Book Two of the Odyssey*

- *Explore the ways in which Homer uses language to engage the audience*

- *Understand the purpose of the polyphonic approach taken in Book Two*

- *Examine the role of Telemachus in the early part of the Odyssey*

- *Begin to consider some of the stylistic techniques used by Homer*

- *Begin to consider some of the linguistic techniques used by Homer*

Book Two of the *Odyssey*

This section will help you to understand the second book of the *Odyssey*. In Book Two Homer continues his telling of the story of Telemachus. He now meets with the people of Ithaca to seek their support for his plan to seek news of his father.

Task: Comprehending Book Two

Read Book Two of the Odyssey

Once you have, write brief responses to the following questions;

- *What has Homer focussed on in Book Two?*
- *How is Telemachus portrayed in Book Two?*
- *Consider why Homer might use such a wide range of speakers in Book Two?*

Book Two: Synopsis

In Book Two of the *Odyssey*, Homer continues with events on Ithaca. Telemachus decides to summon a council of the leading citizens of Ithaca and to inform them of his desire to seek news of Odysseus by travelling to Pylos and Sparta.

Many people speak during the debate, with the older citizens supporting Telemachus in his wishes and the Suitors opposing. A sign is sent by Zeus indicating his support of Telemachus' plans – but this sign is dismissed by the Suitors.

Telemachus returns to the palace and ignoring the veiled and not so veiled threats of the Suitors instructs Eurycleia to prepare his provisions for the journey.

Book Two ends with Athena recruiting a ship and crew for Telemachus and the young hero departs on his journey to Pylos and Sparta.

Characters in Book Two

The following characters are present in Book Two of the Odyssey;

- *Telemachus*
- *Aegyptius*
- *Antinous*
- *Halitherses*
- *Eurymachus*
- *Mentor*
- *Leocritus*
- *Athena (disguised as Mentor)*
- *Unknown Suitors*
- *Eurycleia*

The Structure of Book Two

Book Two of the *Odyssey* can most easily be divided into the following sections;

- Homer sets the scene (lines 1-15)

- The debate at Ithaca (lines 16-260)

- Telemachus and Athena (lines 261-301)

- Telemachus returns to the Palace (lines 302-377)

- Telemachus sets sail (lines 378-434)

Homer sets the scene *(lines 1-15)*

Homer announces Telemachus' intention to summon a council of Ithacans the next morning after the events in Book One. Telemachus dresses and arms himself. Then accompanied by two hounds, Telemachus heads to the assembly he has ordered his heralds to summon. Throughout these fifteen lines Homer deliberately portrays Telemachus as godlike, Athena too casts a glamour over him so that all those Ithacans who witness him marvel at his approach.

The debate at Ithaca (lines 16-260)

Much of the events of Book Two are contained in this section. There are many speakers who contribute to the debate. Telemachus does not speak first. It is Aegyptius, an elder of Ithaca, who speaks first and he has a vested interest in the affairs of Ithaca. One son called Antiphus accompanied Odysseus to Troy and had died at the hands of the Cyclops Polyphemus. Another son named Eurynomus is a Suitor. Two other sons farm the lands. Aegyptius questions the reason why an assembly had been summoned. Was the island under attack?

Telemachus now speaks. He raises two points of business. Odysseus is either dead or still alive and missing. The other point is the damage the Suitors are inflicting on the property of Odysseus. Telemachus demands that the Suitors be restrained from their depredations unless they believe that Odysseus had wronged them. He ends his speech distraught and in tears.

Antonius the leading Suitor now responds. He places the blame for the actions on the Suitors on Penelope. She has deliberately misled them and he recounts the story of the tapestry. He urges that Telemachus make his mother choose a new husband or send her to her father, Icarius, so that he can decide who will marry her.

Telemachus replies. He refuses to send his mother away as this would be disrespectful to both Penelope and the people of Ithaca. Telemachus then prays that the Suitors will be punished by Zeus if they continue in their actions. There is now an interjection from the divine. Zeus sends two eagles to fight over the assembled Ithacans.

This sign is interpreted by Halitherses, a companion of old of Odysseus. He predicts that Odysseus will return soon and urges the Suitors to stop malingering around the palace pestering Penelope and Telemachus. Another suitor, Eurymachus now speaks. He rejects the omen and insists that Odysseus will never return. He accuses Halitherses of encouraging Telemachus to be hostile to the Suitors. Eurymachus urges Telemachus to send Penelope to her father in order that he may choose her a new husband. Until this happens, Eurymachus states that the Suitors will continue in their actions.

Telemachus replies to his audience. He has said enough on the Suitors and now he requests a ship and a crew to enable him to journey to Pylos and Sparta to seek news of Odysseus. If Telemachus hears that Odysseus is dead he will arrange his mother's marriage. If not he will wait for Odysseus to return for another year.

Telemachus is replied to by Mentor, another old comrade of Odysseus. He responds with anger towards the Ithacans, it is *they* who allow the Suitors to act as they do. Mentor is replied to by Leocritus, another Suitor. Leocritus is angry with Mentor's words and declares that Odysseus is dead. In any event, if he is not he states that Odysseus could not defeat so many Suitors. With this lines the assembly disperses.

> **Book Two: The structure of the debate at Ithaca**
>
> - *Aegyptius introduces the debate*
> - *Telemachus states his case*
> - *Antinous replies to Telemachus*
> - *Telemachus responds to Antinous*
> - *Zeus sends a sign*
> - *Halitherses interprets the sign from Zeus*
> - *Eurymachus replies to Halitherses*
> - *Telemachus replies to Eurymachus*
> - *Mentor responds*
> - *Leocritus responds to Mentor*

Telemachus and Athena (lines 261-301)

Telemachus remains in town for the moment. He heads to the sea and entering it, prays to Athena for help. His appeal is successful. Athena disguises herself as Mentor and speaks directly to Telemachus. She declares that Telemachus' journey will be successful, that Telemachus is a true and brave son of Odysseus and that the Suitors are fools who will be punished. She now instructs Telemachus to return to the palace whilst a ship and crew are readied.

> **Book Two: The discussion on the coast**
>
> - *Telemachus prays to Athena*
> - *Athena replies (disguised as Mentor)*

Telemachus returns to the Palace (lines 302-377)

Telemachus returns to the palace. He is greeted by Antinous who perhaps is wary of Telemachus now. He tries to be friendly and offers a crew and a ship. He also asks Telemachus to dine with the Suitors. Telemachus refuses. Perhaps he suspects a trap; that Antinous may try to kill him tonight. This suspicion is reinforced by the statements of two unnamed Suitors; the first says that

Telemachus is seeking aid to help him kill the Suitors, the other hopes that Telemachus goes and is lost at sea.

Telemachus heads through the palace to his rooms, as he goes he calls Eurycleia to him. He instructs this loyal house slave to prepare in secret sufficient food and drink for his journey. Eurycleia is horrified. She does not want Telemachus to go and demonstrates her motherly treatment of Telemachus. For his part, Telemachus replies that he believes a god is helping him. He again instructs Eurycleia to prepare for his departure in secrecy. Penelope in particular should not be told.

Book Two: The discussion in the palace

- *Antinous approaches Telemachus*
- *Telemachus rejects Antinous*
- *Unknown Suitor #1*
- *Unknown Suitor #2*
- *Telemachus speaks to Eurycleia*
- *Eurycleia replies*
- *Telemachus responds*

Telemachus sets sail (lines 378-434)

Homer shifts the action back to Ithaca. Athena, still disguised as Mentor has a ship and crew prepared. Once this is done she goes to Telemachus and informs him to make sail. Telemachus then sets sail.

The Polyphonic nature of Book Two

Given the structure of the second book of the Odyssey, it is clear then that the subject matter of a council of the citizens of Ithaca would lend itself to a whole raft of stylistic techniques that could be utilised by a poet working in the oral tradition.

Poets such as Homer would have used different voices to differentiate between speakers, from loud confident speakers whom the audience might admire (such as Telemachus), to more hesitant voices, or voices of villains (such as the Suitors). These different voices would elicit interest and engagement in the audience and perhaps even add a touch of humour to the performance. At the end of one of his dialogues, Telemachus throws down his staff and sobs; the oral poet would have placed additional emphasis to these words in order to further increase engagement.

Stylistic techniques used by Homer in Book Two

This section focuses on some of the linguistic and stylistic techniques of Homer's *Odyssey*. In particular we will focus on examples drawn from Book Two of the *Odyssey* in order to demonstrate some of these techniques. By introducing some linguistic and stylistic features of the *Odyssey* at this early stage in the guide we will establish a sound basis of understanding of oral composition. When reading Homer, it is important to remember that this epic poem was meant to be **heard**, not read.

Oral poetry is designed to be listened to. As was mentioned earlier, it is almost certain that Homer's poetry comes from a pre-literate period. With one bare exception, there is no mention of writing in either the *Iliad* of or the *Odyssey* and the techniques used in both poems strongly suggest that the poet (or poets) that created these stories was illiterate.

In the ancient world the idea of silent reading was somewhat unusual; typically someone reading a book would read out aloud as they read. When considering the epic poetry of Homer, it is important to bear in mind that the poet would recite and the audience would listen.

Task: The debate at Ithaca

Consider the following aspects in relation to how the characters speak to each other;

- *Subject matter discussed*
- *Language used*
- *How Homer uses this speaker to draw interest*
- *How the elder speakers speak*
- *How the younger speakers speak*
- *The role of the gods in the debate*

Retardation of the plot in Books One and Two

There are several examples of plot retardation in the first few books of the *Odyssey*. There are longer and more noticeable examples to come; some of which will be discussed in later sections. There are some good examples of retardation in the first few books of the *Odyssey* which include;

- ***Book 1, lines 113-119.***

- ***Book 2, lines 270-272 and 278-280***

In this example, Telemachus catches sight of Athena, and the digression involves Telemachus revealing his thoughts, feelings and desires for his father's '*Nostos*' or homecoming.

In the second of these examples, the goddess Athena is disguised as Mentor. Athena converses with Telemachus about the great qualities of Odysseus the hero, these qualities are traits which Telemachus himself has inherited.

These digressions establish Telemachus' status as the true son of Penelope and Odysseus, a hero in waiting, and come before the main thrust of Athena's argument; that Telemachus should seek news of his father.

The Tapestry of Penelope (lines 82-111)

Antinous is used by Homer to provide his audience with another digression. This digression shows that Penelope is reluctant to choose a husband and is capable of her own deceptions. For three years Penelope worked at a tapestry; a funeral sheet for her elderly father. Penelope delayed her Suitors whilst she worked on this tapestry, but each night she unravelled the work she had done that day. Only when the Suitors discovered this trick was Penelope thwarted and forced to complete the tapestry.

Realism in Book Two

Ancient Greeks lived in communities that varied in size but almost all had similar institutions such as the market place (Agora) and the Council (Boule). As such the public meeting summoned by Telemachus in Book Two is in part a realistic portrayal of what a meeting of citizens might have been like in Ancient Greece for a contemporary audience. As such it is a believable and plausible scenario for the Ancient audience, a touch of realism before the story of the *Odyssey* heads into its more fantastical sections – primarily the tale recounted by Odysseus for the Phaeacians in Books nine to twelve. By giving his audience a touch of realism it allows Homer to invite his audience to stretch their imagination to the more fantastic events that occur later in his poem. It also provides a symmetry to the structure of the Iliad; as in that epic poem a council of the Greeks before the walls of Troy is summoned early in that epic poem.

Another vivid description is present at the end of Book Two. Homer describes the boom of the sails and the sounds of the sea as the ship which is carrying Telemachus sets sail.

2.4 Book Three: Nestor

In this section we will;

- *Explore and understand the content and style of Book Three of the Odyssey*

- *Explore the ways in which Homer uses language to engage the audience*

- *Examine the role of Telemachus in the early part of the Odyssey*

- *Explore the role of Nestor in Book Three*

- *Begin to consider the importance of xenia in the Odyssey*

- *Begin to consider some of the stylistic techniques used by Homer*

Book Three of the *Odyssey*

This section will help you to understand the third book of the *Odyssey*. Telemachus arrives at Pylos and seeks the assistance of Nestor.

Task: Comprehending Book Three

Read Book Three of the Odyssey

Once you have, write brief responses to the following questions;

- *What has Homer focussed on in Book Three?*
- *How is Telemachus portrayed in Book Three?*
- *Consider how Telemachus is treated by those he meets in Book Three?*

Book Three: Synopsis

In Book Three Telemachus reaches Pylos. Here he finds the assembled population observing a sacrifice to the God Poseidon. Telemachus and the disguised Athena approach Nestor and his sons and are greeted with food and drink. Athena, still disguised as Mentor offers up a prayer to Poseidon which Telemachus repeats.

After the meal Nestor begins to ask his guests questions – who are they and where are they from? Telemachus answers truthfully – he is Odysseus' son and he is seeking news of his father.

Nestor replies with a story about a feat of Odysseus at Troy. The city had been sacked and many wanted to now return home. Half delayed their sailing with Agamemnon, the other half, including Nestor, Menelaus and Diomedes, set sail immediately. Odysseus first sailed with Nestor, but then returned to Agamemnon. Nestor and Diomedes reached Greece safely, of the rest Nestor knows little.

Telemachus tells Nestor of his troubles back on Ithaca and is informed that surely Athena is watching over him. When Telemachus expresses his doubt about this he is rebuked by the disguised Athena. Telemachus now asks Nestor about the death of Agamemnon and asks where Menelaus was – surely he would have avenged his brother? Nestor replies that Menelaus was swept to Egypt by a fierce storm and has only just returned.

Nestor urges Telemachus to visit Menelaus at Sparta and to help him Nestor provides a chariot and his youngest son Pisistratus as a guide. For the moment though Telemachus is a welcome guest and Athena, seeing that Telemachus has ready allies, reveals herself as she transforms into an eagle and flies away.

The next morning Nestor summons his family and Telemachus' crew and offers a sacrifice to Athena. Telemachus is bathed by Nestor's youngest daughter and then Telemachus and Pisistratus travel by chariot to Sparta.

Characters in Book Three

The following characters are present in Book Three;

- *Telemachus*
- *Athena (disguised as Mentor)*
- *Nestor*
- *Nestor's sons – Thrasymedes, Echephron, Stratius, Persues, Aretus and Pisistratus*
- *Eurydice – Nestor's wife*
- *Polycaste – Nestor's youngest daughter*

The Structure of Book Three

Book Three of the *Odyssey* can most easily be divided into the following sections;

- The feast to Poseidon (lines 1-69)

- Nestor remembers the return from Troy (lines 70-201)

- The stories of Agamemnon and Menelaus (lines 202-328)

- Xenia and departure (lines 329-497)

The feast to Poseidon (lines 1-69)

With the arrival at Pylos, Telemachus is immediately presented with a contrasting display between Pylos and Ithaca. The people of Pylos are numerous and ordered and performing correct sacrifices to the God Poseidon. The choice of Poseidon is also apt for the overall narrative. Not only has Odysseus has angered Poseidon by blinding Polyphemus and it is through this anger that Odysseus is unable to return home, Telemachus too has just completed a sea journey; a sacrifice to the God of the Seas seems therefore appropriate.

Telemachus is hesitant at first; should he just go straight up to King Nestor? What should he say? Athena, still in disguise (though Telemachus already has his suspicions) encourages him and Telemachus allows himself to be persuaded to approach Nestor. The first conversation which involves Nestor is to Athena – he invites her to pray to Poseidon which she does with tact. Telemachus repeats Athena's prayer and the group enjoys a feast.

Nestor remembers the return from Troy (lines 70-201)

Having fed and watered his guests Nestor now asks who they are and where they are from. It is interesting to note that he asks them if they are pirates (line 74-75). His attitude is one of curiosity rather than fear for this particular profession.

Telemachus answers Nestor truthfully – he is Telemachus and he is seeking news of his father. Since Telemachus has responded truthfully, he explicitly requests that Nestor tell him what he knows truthfully as well.

Nestor begins with a litany of some the dead heroes killed at Troy, including Patroclus, Achilles and his own son Antilochus. He then goes on to discuss a quarrel between Menelaus and Agamemnon. Athena had been angered by the Greeks and Menelaus wanted the Greeks to flee home as swift as they could, Agamemnon counselled instead that they try to placate the goddess with sacrifices.

Nestor and Odysseus both chose to depart immediately; however, Odysseus changed his mind and returned to Agamemnon. Nestor and two other leaders of the Greeks, Diomedes and Menelaus continued on. Diomedes and Nestor and their fleets returned to the Peloponnese safely. Of the others, Nestor only heard rumours and these he tells to Telemachus. The son of Achilles, Neoptolemus and Philoctetes returned safely, as did the Cretan King Idomeneus. But Agamemnon was killed as he landed by Aegisthus, only to be avenged later by his son Orestes.

The stories of Agamemnon and Menelaus (lines 202-328)

Telemachus now announces his envy of Orestes and hopes that he too will have the same courage to avenge his father. The talk shifts to the Suitors plaguing Ithaca and Nestor reassures Telemachus that Athena will surely support Telemachus, after all Odysseus was her favourite at Troy. Telemachus doubts this statement and is immediately rebuked by Athena, still in disguise.

Telemachus now invites Nestor to tell him about Menelaus – why did he not avenge Agamemnon? Nestor now tells us part of the story of Aegisthus and Clytemnestra and the reason for Menelaus' absence; he was swept by a storm to Egypt but has now returned. Nestor now advises Telemachus to travel to Sparta and interrogate Menelaus.

Xenia and departure (lines 329-497)

Nestor now offers Telemachus his formal hospitality. He invites him to rest and eat at his palace and set off refreshed in the morning. Nestor himself will keep his crew safe whilst arranging transportation and a guide to lead Telemachus to Sparta. To refuse would be an insult to Nestor and Telemachus is eager to accept.

Seeing that Telemachus is in safe hands Athena reveals herself and departs in the form of an eagle. This reveal is seen as a blessing by Nestor who promises a sacrifice on the morning.

In the morning, Nestor keeps to his promise and sacrifices to Athena with the assistance of his sons. The sacrifice is elaborated on at length by Homer who describes in detail how the horns of the victim are sheathed in gold and the role and function of each son as well as the roles of Nestor's wife and daughters.

Telemachus is absent from the ritual; he is taking a bath and preparing himself for the journey. Once everything is complete Telemachus departs in a chariot accompanied by Nestor's youngest son Pisistratus.

Ritual and sacrifice in Book Three

In Book Three Homer makes begins and ends this part of the Odyssey with scenes of sacrifice. His stories too include references to sacrifices and attempts to appease the god.

How successful is Homer in exploring the importance of piety and sacrifice to the Gods in Book Three?

Xenia in Book Three

The custom and entrenched social value of *Xenia* was so important in which the world outside of one's immediate doorstep was often one fraught with danger and the unknown, and so a fellow Greek-speaker who was far from his home deserved the help and hospitality that any in his position would need. Typically, we see *Xenia* in the *Odyssey* between members of the aristocratic class who honour one another for being fellow aristocrats, but it is certainly a marker of civilisation, of civilized values and of humanity in the *Odyssey*, as shall become apparent later.

In Book Three we see perhaps the most idealised example of *Xenia*; Nestor and his sons invite Telemachus and the disguised Athena to share their meal and prayers before questioning them as to their names and the purpose of their visit. After an exchange of information and advice, Nestor bids his guest farewell and sees Telemachus off in a borrowed chariot filled with gifts and piloted by his son.

Xenia in Book Three

Read the following passages of Homer's *Odyssey*;

- Book III.30-80
- Book III.470-488

These are good examples of the practice of *Xenia* in the early part of the *Odyssey*.

Consider the obligations and courtesies extended by both host and guest.

Since the theme of *Xenia* is commonly examined by the examination boards it is recommended that as many examples of *Xenia* should be explored as possible.

Telemachus' bath? A bath found in the Mycenaean palace at Pylos

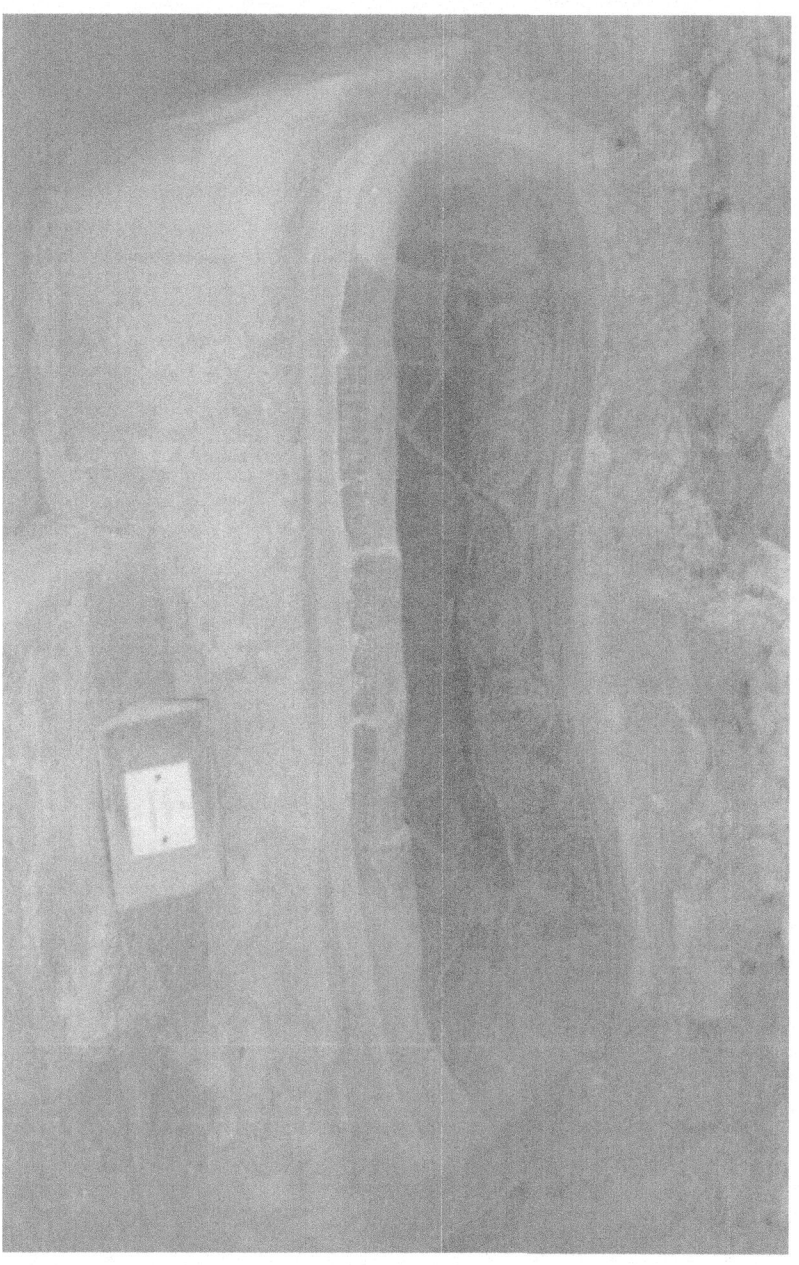

Stylistic techniques used by Homer in Book Three

This section focuses on some of the linguistic and stylistic techniques of Homer's *Odyssey*. In particular we will focus on examples drawn from Book Three of the *Odyssey* in order to demonstrate some of these techniques.

Food and drink in Book Three

Throughout Book Three Homer makes reference to food and drink.

How successful is Homer in exploring the wealth and prosperity of Pylos through portrayal of food and drink in Book Three?

Retardation of the Plot

In Book Three Homer uses a stylistic technique known as retardation of the plot. This means that Homer takes an opportunity to interject a digression into the overall narrative in order to elaborate on a particular point, to develop the personality of a particular character, or it may be that Homer felt the need to extend the length of his poem (remember that Homer is an oral poet performing to a variety of audiences) – it may be that in a particular performance of the *Odyssey* Homer saw then need to extend his tale a little.

This retardation of the plot in Book Three takes the form of a digression. Nestor is speaking and he is talking about Odysseus. Rather than just tell Telemachus that he does not know where Odysseus is, Homer uses Nestor's voice to tell a tale of the heroes returning from Troy. It could be that Homer is developing his character of Nestor, Nestor is an old venerable king, a veteran of many a military campaign and like many an old soldier across time and literature, Nestor could be eager to use this opportunity to reminisce about the war at Troy and his friends and comrades there.

The litany of the fallen Greek heroes in lines 109-111 is also part of this retardation. However here Nestor is also remembering not only dead comrades such as Achilles, but his own son Antilochus who was killed by Memnon, the son of Morning in a battle after the events described in the Iliad. This example, along with others in Book Four, help the audience to remember that the *Tale of Troy* contained many interconnected episodes that went beyond what is recorded in the *Iliad* and that poets such as Homer, and their Greek audiences where familiar with a much rich and extensive canon of Greek myths and legends that helped to explain their past, culture and origins.

2.5 Book Four: Menelaus and Storytelling

In this section we will;

- *Explore and understand the content and style of Book Four of the Odyssey*

- *Explore the ways in which Homer uses language to engage the audience*

- *Understand the role and purposes of storytelling in the Odyssey*

- *Consider the parallels between Menelaus and Odysseus*

- *Examine the role of Telemachus in the early part of the Odyssey*

- *Consider the use of simile in the Odyssey*

Book Four of the *Odyssey*

This section will help you to understand the fourth book of the *Odyssey*. This book is one of the longer sections of the Odyssey and it is here that Homer reveals some news to Telemachus of the fate of his father.

> **Task: Comprehending Book Four**
>
> *Read Book Four of the Odyssey*
>
> *Once you have, write brief responses to the following questions;*
>
> - *What has Homer focussed on in Book Four?*
> - *How crucial to the overall narrative are the events of Book Four?*
> - *How are characters like Menelaus and Helen portrayed?*

Book Four: Synopsis

The final book of the *Telemachy*, is Book Four. Telemachus and Peisistratus reach Sparta, the home of Menelaus and Helen. This couple have only recently returned home, like Odysseus, Menelaus was also delayed in his return journey from Troy.

Telemachus arrives during wedding festivities; Menelaus and Helen are celebrating the marriage of their children. Despite potentially interrupting the wedding, Menelaus welcomes his visitors and offers them his hospitality.

He entertains them with food, drink and several stories in his opulent palace that is filled with wealth and splendour. Like Nestor in Book Three, Menelaus regales his guests with stories of his comrades from the Trojan war, referring to his sorrow at the fate of Agamemnon; killed by his wife Clytemnestra and her lover.

Menelaus does not know who Telemachus is, rather it is for Helen to reveal the identity of Telemachus. Emotions run high with the sorrowful stories and so Helen drugs her guests in order to purge them of their grief and as she does, she tells an anecdote of Odysseus' bravery and heroic actions at Troy. Menelaus too also gives an anecdote of Odysseus and his bravery in the final battle that saw Troy destroyed. With these stories complete, they all retire to sleep.

It is only the morning of the following day that Menelaus asks Telemachus questions – who are they and where are they from? Telemachus answers truthfully – he is Odysseus' son and he is seeking news of his father. Menelaus then tells Telemachus of his own journey home. He was delayed in Egypt, but whilst there he learns from the Old Man of the Sea of the fate of several comrades slain since the fall of Troy; he also reveals news that Odysseus is not dead, but he is a prisoner of the nymph Calypso.

The end of Book Four sees Homer shift the story back to Ithaca. Here he reveals that the Suitors finally discover that Telemachus has left the island and they conspire to ambush and kill him at sea. Penelope too discovers that her son is gone and fears for his safety. Athena however sends a phantom to reassure Penelope that Telemachus is safe.

The Structure of Book One

Book Four is the longest of the *Odyssey* and contains several distinct sections

- Arrival in Sparta (lines 1-120)

- The stories of Helen and Menelaus (lines 121-305)

- The second introduction (lines 306-350)

- Menelaus' story (lines 351-624)

- Ithaca (lines 625-end)

Characters in Book Four

The following characters are present in Book Four of the Odyssey;

- *Telemachus*

- *Peisistratus*

- *Eteoneus, steward of Menelaus*

- *Menelaus*

- *Helen*

- *Noemon, a ship owner*

- *Antinous, a leading suitor*

- *Medon, a loyal herald*

- *Eurycleia, a loyal household slave*

- *Penelope*

- *Iphthime, phantom of Penelope's sister*

Arrival in Sparta (lines 1-120)

Telemachus and Peisistratus arrive in Sparta to scenes of a wedding celebration. Menelaus and Helen's daughter Hermione is to be sent off to marry Achilles' son Neoptolemus, whilst Menelaus' son Megapenthes was marrying a local Spartan girl.

> **Task: Comparing Menelaus and Nestor**
>
> Write brief responses to the following questions;
>
> List the similarities and differences are there between Homer's portrayal of the characters of Menelaus and Nestor.
>
> Likewise consider the similarities and differences between how Homer sets the scenes in Pylos and Sparta.

Eteoneus, the squire of Menelaus, asks what to do. Should Telemachus be offered hospitality? Menelaus replies that these strangers should be granted the fullest extent of hospitality. After all, they themselves received the same whilst on their travels.

Telemachus and Peisistratus enter the palace and marvel at the splendour and wealth of the place. Homer does this intentionally, as he wants to convey a comparison between the palace of Menelaus and the palace of Odysseus in its present state. Menelaus' home is how Odysseus' palace *should* be. It is the presence of the suitors that are ruining the wealth and prestige of the place.

For Telemachus, Menelaus' home looks like the home of a God. When this contrast is commented on by Telemachus however, Menelaus is quick to deny it. He has no desire to incur the hostility of the Gods and Homer uses the opportunity this affords to have Menelaus digress briefly on his travels to Egypt, Cyprus, Libya and Ethiopia as well as to introduce his sorrow for the loss of his brother Agamemnon and other heroes from the Trojan War.

The stories of Helen and Menelaus (lines 121-305)

Book Four includes several examples of storytelling. A pair of stories are told by Helen and Menelaus and the subject matter of these stories are the heroic activities of Odysseus at Troy.

Helen is brought into the narrative by Homer at this point and the poet illustrates her arrival with a digression on her 'silver work basket', a gift given by Alcandre, the wife of Polybus (lines 124-138). It is Helen that reveals the identity of Telemachus to Menelaus – the boy resembles his father. Despite this revelation, Telemachus remains silent and it is his comrade Peisistratus that speaks on his behalf and announces the purpose for their visit.

Menelaus in turn announces his great friendship with Odysseus, stating how he'd like to move Odysseus to Sparta so that they could be neighbours. Peisistratus requests from Menelaus stories of events at Troy and comrades lost, after all Peisistratus himself lost a brother there – Antilochus.

Helen's story (lines 239-264) describes how Odysseus used his skill at disguise to sneak into Troy and spy on the enemy. Helen was the only person to see through the disguise and helped him to escape. As he left Troy he did so in scenes of mayhem; slaying many Trojans on his way out.

Menelaus continues this eulogy of Odysseus by expressing his admiration of Odysseus' courage in a moment of great stress (lines 265-289). Hiding in the great wooden horse that has been dragged into the city, the Greek warriors are sorely tested by the voice of the Trojan Deiphobus. It is Odysseus that forced Menelaus and Diomedes to remain calm and not give away their hiding place in the wooden horse and then accompanied Menelaus in the battle that followed.

Task: The portrayal of a hero

For Homer, the key to being a hero was the desire for *timé* and the concern for their future *kleos*.

Why might these stories be crucial for portraying Odysseus before this character is introduced in Book Five?

These stories are a source of both pride and sorrow for those present and it is Helen who uses this opportunity to drug Menelaus, Peisistratus and Telemachus and wash away their grief.

The second introduction (lines 306-350)

Homer now has his characters sleep. When Telemachus wakes he is greeted by Menelaus who now asks; who are they and where are they from? Telemachus answers truthfully – he is Odysseus' son and he is seeking news of his father.

This is odd. After all, Telemachus has already been in the presence of Menelaus all of the previous night and he already knows who he is and why he is in his house!

Telemachus in turn responds to Menelaus' questions by recounting his problems with the Suitors to Menelaus (lines 315-332).

Menelaus' reply is characteristic;

'Auburn-haired Menelaus was hot with indignation. How disgraceful!' he cried.

'So the cowards want to creep into the brave man's bed?'

Book IV.333-335

The descriptive *'auburn-haired'* is used for Menelaus. This description was characteristic of Menelaus and used in the *Iliad* as well as the *Odyssey*.

According to Greek legend Menelaus was red-headed, and the Greeks customarily thought of him as hot-tempered. In the ancient world of the Greeks red-hair with sometimes considered as imparting a rash or hot headed temperament. In this context the use of this descriptive serves to remind the audience that Menelaus possesses an angry character by nature.

This is belief is compounded by the next particularly vivid outburst, *'So the cowards want to creep into the brave man's bed!'* By putting these words into Menelaus' mouth, Homer is doing this for a particular reason. It serves to remind Homer's audience of the scandalous, even criminal nature of the Suitors' intentions. Not only do they want to Odysseus' home, his household goods and his riches, but they also intend to steal Odysseus' wife.

The disgust of Menelaus is clearly apparent; the bravery of Odysseus has been contrasted with the cowardice of the Suitors.

Task: Analysing a Homeric simile

> *"Auburn haired Menelaus was hot with indignation. 'How disgraceful! He cried. 'So the cowards want to creep into the brave man's bed? It's just as if a deer had put her two little unweaned fawns to sleep in a mighty lion's den and gone to range the high ridges and grassy dales for pasture. Back comes the lion to his lair, and the fawns meet a grisly fate – as will the* Suitors at Odysseus' hand."

> Homer's *Odyssey* Book IV. 331-340

Ensure that you are able to write a brief response to the following question;

What is the subject of the simile in this passage?

What do you think the effect of this simile is here?

How effective do you think it is in conveying an image to the audience?

Menelaus' simile (lines 331-340)

The similes used by Homer are typically extensions of the previous sentence. In the above example, the simile serves to contrast between the bravery of Odysseus against the cowardly nature of the Suitors. The animal comparison between the predator; the lion, and the prey; the deer, is particularly apt. Odysseus is destined to hunt down the Suitors on his return to Ithaca and Menelaus assumes *will* happen and will take just revenge for their behaviour; as is appropriate for a Homeric hero.

Menelaus and Proteus (lines 351-624):

<table>
<tr><td>

Remember

Similes and exam style responses

Examination boards routinely include passages that have similes.

If the passage in the exam includes a simile – point it out and consider its effectiveness.

</td></tr>
</table>

After demonstrating his disgust with the Suitors, Menelaus continues the story of his own wanderings after the Trojan War. Menelaus recounts his travels in the eastern Mediterranean including his stay in Egypt.

Menelaus' tale is comparable to Nestor's story in Book 3. Since Telemachus' journey is essentially motivated by his desire to find out about where Odysseus might be, and he does this by listening to his father's friends' stories, of which this is one. It is unsurprising to find that Homer uses story-telling as the primary medium for conveying this information to Telemachus.

Menelaus' story includes the elements of the natural and the supernatural. He has already describes how he cruised around the eastern Mediterranean where he visited historical peoples. Menelaus also tells Telemachus how he captured and forced the Old Man of the Sea in order to tell him how to return to Sparta. Such stories prepare the audience to expect such features in other stories in future, particularly those of Odysseus, and remind the audience that such extraordinary events were not unusual occurrences for heroes of Greek Myth.

> *Menelaus and Proteus*
>
> *Structure of story;*
>
> - *Lines 350-459: How to catch Proteus*
> - *Lines 460-498 How Menelaus will get home*
> - *Lines 499-511 the fate of Ajax*
> - *Lines 512-549 the fate of Agamemnon*
> - *Lines 550-561 the fate of Odysseus*
> - *Lines 562-569 the fate of Menelaus*

Menelaus informs Telemachus that he was trapped by the Gods in Egypt. However, at the instruction of the Goddess Eidothae, Menelaus determines to capture her father, Proteus, the Old Man of the Sea and force him to tell Menelaus of the God that is preventing him from setting sail. Menelaus and some of his men disguise themselves as seals on the beach were Proteus comes ashore.

Once they have him in their sights, Menelaus jumps up and wrestles the shape shifting Proteus to the ground and holds him in place until he surrenders. Proteus submits to Menelaus and tells him it was improper sacrifice that keeps him from setting sail. Then Menelaus asks news of his comrades from the Trojan War, (lines 481-586,) he is told of the deaths of 'Little' Ajax and Agamemnon and that Odysseus is a prisoner.

Telling stories within stories is a favourite feature of Homer's, and is certainly a type of digression. Time and again this occurs in the *Odyssey,* the Books Nine to Twelve being the longest example.

Book Four of the Odyssey

At over 800 lines, Book Four is one of the longer episodes in the Odyssey. In brief, the action of Book 4 can be divided as follows;

- *The arrival of Telemachus and Peisistratus at Sparta.*

- *Introductions and grief for the missing and dead by Menelaus, Peisistratus and Telemachus.*

- *Stories recounting the heroic deeds of Odysseus at Troy by Helen and Menelaus.*

- *Telemachus explains his reason for visiting to Menelaus.*

- *Menelaus' recounts his encounter with Proteus.*

- *The Suitors conspire at Ithaca.*

- *Penelope learns that the Suitors plot to kill Telemachus.*

The return to Ithaca in Book Four (lines 625-end)

The return to events on Ithaca allows the audience to observe what is occurring in the absence of Telemachus. In the final part of Book Four, Homer is establishing what Ithaca is like without either Odysseus *or* Telemachus, and how Penelope cannot cope at all when she is entirely on her own.

The ship owner Noemon arrives at the palace. Approaching the suitors he wants to know when Telemachus will return with his ship as he wants to use it.

Discovering Telemachus is away, the Suitors determine that Telemachus may become a threat, and decide to ambush and kill him at sea. However, the loyal herald Medon overhears Antinous and hurries away to tell Penelope that her son has sailed away and that Telemachus is in danger from the Suitors.

Penelope being told this is distraught and raises a lament (lines 722-741). Eurycleia reveals what she knows of Telemachus' absence and the purpose of his travel. However Penelope remains in distress. It is Athena who sends a spirit to comfort Penelope, without telling her of Odysseus' fate.

The return to Ithaca also allows the audience to see the Suitors for what they are. Dishonest and murderous in their intentions, they do not present a positive picture of themselves at all. The pictured presented of Ithaca therefore is one of chaos. Odysseus needs to return to bring order to this chaos and he needs to return soon

---

Point to consider

As you read Book four of the *Odyssey*, consider the change in scene from Sparta to Ithaca.

What do you think the purpose of this change in scene is?

Task: Examination style questions

A level Commentary- Style Questions

Having read Book 4 and considered some of the structural features important to the narrative, it is now time to consider as examination style commentary question. Each examination board uses 'set texts' from which they use excerpts from Homer and set a series of questions relating to the passage.

In the examination, you will be expected to comment on the language Homer uses to produce a particular effect in a reprinted passage from the set text.

Book 4 is commonly used by the examination boards to supply these commentary style questions. You are encouraged to study those set text sections in more depth and detail, paying close attention to the language and styles used and the effect it is intended to convey.

In the following task box is an examination-style question. This question requires that you consider the choice of *words* Homer has made and the events he chooses to describe;

Read Book IV.460- 488

From; *"When at last the old man who knew so many tricks grew wary, he broke into speech and began asking me questions..."*

To; *"But there is a third who, though still alive, is a prisoner somewhere in the vastness of the seas."*

Questions

    a) Describe briefly what has occurred in the events preceding this excerpt.

    b) How effectively does Homer convey tension in this passage? In your answer you should consider the language Homer uses.

    c) Using this passage as a starting point, How typical is this passage in demonstrating storytelling in the *Odyssey*?

Part Three: Odysseus among the Phaeacians

Part Three: Odysseus among the Phaeacians

3.1 Book Five: Odysseus and the Gods

3.2 Book Six: Nausicaa

3.3 Book Seven: The Phaeacians - Realism and fantasy

3.4 Book Eight: *Xenia* and the Heroic Code

Odysseus Among the Phaeacians

In Books 5-8 of the *Odyssey*, Homer now directs the focus of his story to Odysseus. Odysseus is a prisoner of Calypso on the island of Ogygia. After being a rather unwilling guest of Calypso for seven years the Olympian Zeus at last orders the release of Odysseus and sends Hermes to Ogygia to issue these commands.

Odysseus builds a raft and sets sail and after many days sailing reaches sight of land, however his smooth journey is thrown into turmoil by Poseidon, who spots Odysseus and whips up a storm. Odysseus' raft is wrecked and Odysseus is saved from drowning by the intervention of the Goddesses Ino and also Athena. Odysseus reaches land, but does so naked and exhausted.

Odysseus has reached Scherie, the island of the Phaeacians. The Phaeacians are a semi-mythical race of mortals who have blessings far in excess of all other humans. Odysseus is happened upon by the princess Nausicaa and Odysseus uses a combination of charm and desperation to convince Nausicaa to provide assistance. Nausicaa directs Odysseus to her city and instructs the hero to seek the help of her mother Arete.

Reaching the palace disguised in a mist conjured by Athena who directs him through the city of the Phaeacians, Odysseus reaches the palace and supplicates himself before Arete. At first the Phaeacians are taken aback by Odysseus' sudden appearance, but they immediately offer him good *xenia* and the Phaeacian lord Alcinous offers to transport Odysseus to wherever he wills.

Whilst the ship is being prepared the Phaeacians demonstrate their prowess in a variety of sporting activities. One Phaeacian taunts Odysseus, who angered, throws a discus far beyond what the others are capable of. The Phaeacians return to the palace for a feast and listen to stories of the Trojan War. These tales cause Odysseus grief and at the pressing of Alcinous, Odysseus agrees to tell the story of his travels.

3.1 Book Five: Odysseus and the Gods

In this section we will;

- *Explore and understand the content and style of Book Five of the Odyssey*

- *Consider the role of the power of fate in the Odyssey*

- *Explore the role of the immortals in the Odyssey*

- *Begin to consider the relationship between immortals and mortals in the Odyssey*

- *Begin to explore the character and personality of Odysseus*

- *Explore some of the linguistics techniques used by Homer*

Book Five of the *Odyssey*

This section will help you to understand the fifth book of the *Odyssey*. In Book Five Homer finally introduces his audience to the main protagonist of his story; Odysseus.

Task: Comprehending Book Five

Read Book Five of the Odyssey

Once you have, write brief responses to the following questions;

- *What has Homer focussed on in Book Five?*
- *How is Odysseus is portrayed in Book Five?*
- *Consider the role of the Gods in Book Five and their relationship with Odysseus?*

Book Five: Synopsis

In Book Five of the *Odyssey* Homer is primarily concerned with presenting Odysseus as the victim and plaything of the Gods. Odysseus has spent the last seven years as the 'guest' of Calypso. He was washed up on this isolated island as the sole survivor of a shipwreck. Despite the paradisiacal nature of Calypso's island and the offer of become her permanent (and immortal) consort, Odysseus still remains full of sick and longing for his home on Ithaca and desires above all else to return to his family.

This book starts with a scene of the Gods, with Zeus instructing Hermes to go to Calypso's island and order the Nymph to release Odysseus. Calypso obeys the instructions sent from Zeus with some reluctance and helps Odysseus prepare for the long journey across the sea.

Odysseus sets sail on a raft and after many days sailing sees at last the island of Scherie; the home of the Phaeacians. However it is at this point when Poseidon spots Odysseus' raft and determined to make life difficult for Odysseus whips up a storm.

Odysseus' raft is wrecked and the hero must swim for shore, hindered by Poseidon on the one hand and helped by the Goddesses Athena and Ino on the other. Odysseus finally reaches land, but does so in almost as sorry a state as he was when he was first encountered. He is battered, bruised and naked in a strange land.

Characters in Book Five

The following characters are present in Book Five of the Odyssey;

- *Odysseus*
- *Zeus*
- *Athena*
- *Hermes*
- *Calypso*
- *Poseidon*
- *Ino*

The Structure of Book Five

Book Five of the *Odyssey* can most easily be divided into the following sections;

- The Gods *(lines 1-149)*

- Odysseus and Calypso *(lines 150-268)*

- The Storm *(lines 269-380)*

- Odysseus reaches land *(381-end)*

The Gods *(lines 1-149)*

Homer commences Book Five with the Gods. Athena calls upon Zeus to bring about the return of Odysseus to Ithaca. Homer then has returned us to almost the very beginning of the *Odyssey*; when Zeus permits Athena to visit Telemachus and likewise promises to send Hermes to order the release of Odysseus. Athena has duly dispatched Telemachus to Nestor and Menelaus, and now Zeus instructs Hermes to set out.

Hermes travels across the seas to the island of Calypso in some detail. In lines 50-58 Homer uses a simile to describe the approach of Hermes to the island. He is skimming the waves like a swooping seagull, pursuing fish in the sea.

Homer continues with a vivid description of Calypso's home. Calypso is singing at home weaving and her home is a fragrant cave sheltered by different kinds of trees suitable for the construction of sea faring vessels and these trees are the home of many birds. Close nearby is a vineyard, a meadow and four small rivers with clear crystal waters. The picture being drawn by Homer is a paradise; a fine balance of nature and civilisation.

Hermes is greeted by Calypso and offered her hospitality; a chair, food and drink. Only once he has partaken of this hospitality does Hermes explain the reason for his visit.

Hermes states that Zeus has ordered her to release Odysseus. He is destined to reach Ithaca. Calypso agrees to obey, but she is not happy about it. She complains that the male Gods have double standards; *they* can fool about with mortal women as much as they

Hermes' journey

Read Book V.43-73 of the Odyssey

What linguistic techniques can be identified in these lines?

How does Homer describe the island of Calypso as seen by Hermes?

want to, but a female Goddess who does the same causes outrage.

Odysseus and Calypso *(lines 150-268)*

Odysseus enters the *Odyssey* from lines 149 onwards in Book Five. Although Calypso has been instructed to set him free, Odysseus is first encountered sitting on the beach, crying, with reddened eyes. Odysseus is first encountered by the audience in an extremely pitiable state, at the bottom of the pit of despair. It is not quite the 'heroic' entrance we might have expected from such a description and one that contrasts with the first impressions that we encounter of the hero Achilles in the *Iliad*. Homer introduces a little touch of humour and *pathos* when he first introduces Odysseus. Odysseus then is presented to us as a very humane character.

Odysseus has clearly been much reduced after so many sufferings that he has encountered. These sufferings have not yet been revealed to the audience but await description through Books Nine to Twelve.

> **Pathos**
>
> *Pathos is* the term used to describe a scene that elicits sympathy and or pity in the audience.

However, Odysseus' basic character traits can still be identified. At first he suspects a trick but upon being assured by Calypso he begins to demonstrate his abilities and will. He is clearly a man of resource, able to build a raft once Calypso has allowed him to leave, and certainly courteous and tactful since he manages to assuage Calypso's jealousy and displeasure at his leaving with tact and politeness.

Book 5 very much marks a departure from the first 4 Books; the so called *'Telemachy'* of the *Odyssey*. Whilst Odysseus has been mentioned through the *'Telemachy'*, the main protagonist of the poem has been absent so far. It is now in Book Five that Homer begins to focus on the hero.

As is clearly apparent in Book Five, Odysseus is a far sight from the idealised hero that is portrayed in the *Iliad*. So far in the first four books; Odysseus has been described as a great man, a king amongst men; he has been likened to as a lion by, Menelaus, and his absence from Ithaca is amply demonstrated by the chaos in his household.

Task: The presentation of character in Book Five.

Read Book Five of the *Odyssey*.

Complete the following table, recording examples from Book Five of how Homer presents Calypso and Odysseus. Consider the language used by Homer to describe these characters.

Calypso in book 5	Odysseus in book 5

However, by the end of Book Five Odysseus finds himself once more the helpless victim of a God's anger. Poseidon destroys his raft and determines to drown him. Odysseus survives to be washed up on another island, exhausted, half drowned and his hopes once again dashed.

The Storm *(lines 269-380)*

Odysseus sets sail on a raft he has constructed himself. He is clothed and provided with food and drink by Calypso and for seventeen days he sails without incident. On the 18th day he spies in the distance the island of Scherie; the home of the Phaeacians. At the same time however the God Poseidon spots him. Poseidon is angered by the actions of his fellow gods – who have set Odysseus on his way whilst Poseidon was absent in Ethiopia. Poseidon realises he cannot prevent Odysseus from returning to Ithaca, but he can give him a difficult time. A storm erupts which throws Odysseus into despair (lines 299-313).

Homer uses vivid language to describe the storm. The waves are described as mountainous; the sea like brine and the raft is destroyed in some detail. In lines 329-333 Homer uses a simile to describe the power of the winds.

Odysseus is not entirely alone however. The Goddess Ino (also known as Leucothae) see Odysseus and, taking the form of a gull, gives him instruction. Odysseus is to strip off his clothes that are weighing him down and to swim to shore carrying only the veil which the goddess gives him. Once ashore he is to return the veil by casting it into the sea.

Odysseus however is sceptical. He suspects a trick (as he did earlier with Calypso). So Odysseus remains with what is left of his raft for two days. Other waves sent by Poseidon buffet Odysseus and his raft, giving Homer the opportunity to use more similes (lines 364-375) to describe the situation Odysseus finds himself in.

Odysseus reaches land *(381-end)*

Poseidon leaves Odysseus astride what is left of his raft content with the knowledge that Odysseus has suffered some more adversity and Athena is able to calm the waves and dispel the storm. What follows is an analogy by Homer (lines 390-398) in which Homer presents Odysseus' relief at surviving the storm much as a family rejoices when they discover that their sick father will recover from his illness. Odysseus draws near to Scherie.

However Odysseus still has problems. He cannot find a way to get onto the island. The island is a very rocky one and the waves crash against the shore. Athena comes to Odysseus' difference. She guides him to grab for the rocks – which results in the use of another simile by Homer;

'Pieces of skin stripped from his sturdy hands were left sticking to the crag, like the pebbles that stick to the suckers of a squid when it is torn from its lair'

Book V. 431-436

Odysseus enters into a river with a prayer for the spirit of the place to let him pass unimpeded. This he does and finally Odysseus reaches land. He returns the veil of Ino but he is still in despair. He is exhausted and scared of the cold and wild animals of this unfamiliar place. But Odysseus does what he needs to do; he goes to sleep, concealed in a pile of leaves.

The Gods in the *Odyssey* in Books Five: The role of the gods and the power of fate

In many Ancient Greek plays and poems, the gods have an important role to play in directing events although as Zeus says at the beginning of Book One in the *Odyssey*, man still retains direct responsibility for his actions. There are many examples of this responsibility in Ancient Greek plays and poems, from the actions of Achilles that cause such grief for the Greeks before Troy, including to himself by the loss of his great friend Patroclus to the example of Aegisthus who, not content with adultery, killed Agamemnon despite being warned by Hermes not to commit these crimes.

The Greeks thought of their gods and divines as having as human characters and personalities, complete with their own strengths and weaknesses: this allows them to interact with each other and with the humanity in a very human way.

The relationships that gods and mortals have with each other are a key theme in the *Odyssey*.

The Olympian gods are key characters in the *Odyssey*. In Book one for example, the gods meet in council and the audience are introduced to two of the gods important in the *Odyssey*, and indeed in Ancient Greek religious beliefs, Athena and her father Zeus. Taking advantage of the absence of Poseidon, her uncle, Athena discusses her plans for Odysseus. As the patron of Odysseus, Athena is keen to help Odysseus return home to Ithaca. Poseidon on the other hand hates Odysseus for reasons of his own, which will become apparent to the audience later on in the *Odyssey*.

Calypso

Another character of some importance is introduced in Book Five. Calypso, unlike Hermes, Zeus and Athena is not an Olympian God; she does not dwell on Mount Olympus but instead has made the island where Odysseus is marooned her home, along with her attendant nymphs. Calypso then is a minor Goddess with much less power and influence than any of the Olympian Gods. In Ancient Greek religion there major Olympian deities were worshipped along with countless local spirits and gods associated with islands, rivers, springs, mountains and so forth. Calypso belongs in this group of Gods.

Although Calypso only appears in this Book Five of the *Odyssey*, she is important nevertheless since she has been responsible for the longest delay in Odysseus' journey home. For seven years Odysseus has been kept as a plaything of Calypso and is unable to escape.

It is possible to feel some sympathy for Calypso. Despite her attendant Nymphs, she is clearly lonely on her island and has taken advantage of Odysseus' plight to rectify this loneliness. She has therefore kept Odysseus trapped on her island and she has denied him the opportunity to leave. In this Calypso has acted selfishly, as a God was expected to do. The needs and desires of a mortal clearly in this case do not count.

Despite being immortal, Calypso is otherwise depicted as a woman. For example she enjoys singing and weaving as mortal women in the *Odyssey* do. She dislikes being ordered around by Zeus via Hermes, and reluctantly accepts the superior power of Zeus who wills Odysseus to leave, though not without some petulance; the attitude presented by Homer is somewhat similar to a stubborn daughter defying her Father for a time before obeying.

Once Hermes has departed, she presents the will of Zeus as if it is her own idea. This deceit is designed to save her own embarrassment. Again, this action is typically human.

> **Task: Calypso**
>
> Write several paragraphs on the character of Calypso.
>
> Consider;
>
> - Homer's use of language used in describing both her and her island.
> - Her interactions with both Hermes and Zeus.
> - Her interaction with Odysseus.

Calypso and the use and abuse of *xenia*

Calypso demonstrates both positive and negative *xenia* in these lines; on the one hand Calypso shows good *xenia* towards the God Hermes, however she has also abused the laws of hospitality by denying Odysseus the right to leave her island for many years. When Calypso agrees to release Odysseus he refuses to believe her considering her to be playing tricks on him.

> **Remember!**
>
> The Greeks thought of their gods and divines as having as human characters and personalities, complete with their own foibles: this allows them to interact with each other and with the human characters in a very human-like way.

Task: Examination style response

Write a response to the following question;

"How far do you agree with the view that Odysseus as portrayed in Book Five has neither Honour (timé) nor Reputation (kleos)?"

Treat this question as an examination style question. As such you will need to arrive at a judgement on the representation contained in the question. You will need to find evidence that will either challenge or support the argument that you put forward.

3.2 Book Six: Nausicaa

In this section we will;

- Explore and understand the content and style of Book Six of the Odyssey

- Consider the role of women in the Odyssey

- Compare the characters of Nausicaa and Calypso

- Explore the character and personality of Odysseus

- Explore some of the linguistics techniques used by Homer

Book Six of the *Odyssey*

This topic will help you to understand the sixth book of the *Odyssey*. This section examines the role of women in the *Odyssey*. In this topic we will examine the character of Nausicaa

In comparison to the *Iliad*, where the focus of events is very much concerned with the actions of the warriors fighting in the Trojan War, the *Odyssey* has a greater range of female characters that have a greater influence on events that occur. Nausicaa is a character of importance In Book Six; but she seldom appears elsewhere in the Odyssey.

Task: Comprehending Book Six

Read Book Six of the Odyssey

Once you have, write brief responses to the following questions;

- *What has Homer focussed on in Book Six?*
- *How is Nausicaa portrayed in Book Six?*
- *How is Odysseus portrayed in Book Six?*

Book Six: Synopsis

In Book Six Odysseus makes contact with the Phaeacian princess Nausicaa, who directs him to her city and provides him with information on how best to approach her parents for help. Homer continues in Book Six to present Odysseus as the victim and plaything of the Gods and a man in need of help.

Characters in Book Six

The following characters are present in Book Six of the Odyssey;

- *Odysseus*
- *Nausicaa, a Phaeacian Princess*
- *Athena*
- *Alcinous, the lord of the Phaeacians*

The Structure of Book Six

Book Six of the *Odyssey* can most easily be divided into the following sections;

- The origins of the Phaeacians *(lines 1-15)*

- Nausicaa *(lines 16-109)*

- Nausicaa and Odysseus *(lines 110-250)*

- Nausicaa's instructions to Odysseus *(251-end)*

The origins of the Phaeacians *(lines 1-15)*

Homer spends a short amount of time clarifying for his audience the origin of the Phaeacian people. They are presented as inhabitants of an idyllic land, but also as colonists. The Phaeacians moved from their homeland (a land close to the land of the Cyclopes) because of the predations of their neighbours and moved to the island of Scherie – the place where Odysseus had been washed ashore.

Nausicaa *(lines 16-109)*

Homer introduces a new character in Book Six. Nausicaa is a Phaeacian princess, the daughter of their lord Alcinous. She is visited in the night by the goddess Athena, who is disguised as Dymae, a friend of Nausicaa.

Nausicaa is something of a unique character in the *Odyssey*. Whilst Penelope is Odysseus' wife and Calypso is the goddess that has taken Odysseus as her lover as well as her prisoner, Nausicaa is a young princess, but nevertheless she is strong and decisive.

Whilst Book 5 is in some ways the book of Calypso, Book Six is Nausicaa's book. Together they form a natural counterpoint to each other.

Task: Nausicaa

Read Book Six

Explore the character and role of Nausicaa.

Consider;

- The use of language that Homer uses in portraying Nausicaa.

- The way in which she interacts with her maids.

Athena instructs Nausicaa to tidy herself up and wash her clothes in preparation of marriage, as she will surely soon find a suitable husband. This at first might seem a somewhat strange motivation, but Homer uses the idea of washing her best clothes in order to get Nausicaa out of the palace and down to the river in order so that she can meet Odysseus.

By also implanting the idea of marriage into the head of Nausicaa, Athena is also influencing Nausicaa so that she might look upon Odysseus as potential marriage material when she encounters him. In other words, the stage is being set to make Nausicaa help Odysseus.

Nausicaa gathers her maids and requests a cart to transport her laundry to the river. Homer then paints a tranquil scene of Nausicaa and her maids washing their clothes, playing a ball game and eating a picnic. Nearby, Odysseus sleeps in the bushes.

Nausicaa and Odysseus *(lines 110-250)*

Odysseus is awakened by the maids at play. At first he fears for his safety. Has he landed on an island of savages? Given his previous experiences (that will be recounted in Books Nine to Twelve), these fears are understandable. However, his curiosity overcomes this fear and he investigates.

Homer likens Odysseus' approach to the maids as to that of a stalking mountain lion in a simile (lines 129-138) and his appearance startles Nausicaa and her maids. Whilst the maids scatter, Nausicaa stands her ground.

Odysseus immediately turns on his charm. He flatters Nausicaa and her maids and asks for help. Nausicaa is willing to help. She clothes Odysseus and feeds him, in part she is influenced by Athena who makes Odysseus seem 'like a God'. This attracts the princess.

Nausicaa's instructions to Odysseus *(251-end)*

Nausicaa instructs Odysseus to follow her and the maids when they return to the city. However she does not want him to accompany her directly. Instead she instructs Odysseus to wait in a small woodland give that is sacred to Athena and allow Nausicaa time to reach the palace. Odysseus should then enter the city and when he enters the palace he should make his appeal directly to Nausicaa's mother – not her father.

The Book ends with Odysseus following Nausicaa as far as the sacred grove. Here he prays to Athena to help him. However, his prayer expresses some resentment to the goddess that she has not helped before. Athena however hears his prayer, but Homer expressly says that she does not reveal herself to Odysseus – due to the continued hostility of her Uncle; the God of the Sea Poseidon.

In this section Nausicaa is imagining what others will say of her, and in this way distances herself from what she really thinks by putting these opinions into the mouths of others.

Nausicaa is shy and demure, however she is clearly attracted to Odysseus, yet it would not be acceptable to declare her feelings outright. However, she does not fail to hint about her feelings, such as when she says: *'Who is this tall and handsome stranger with Nausicaa?'* (lines 276-277).

In fact, talking about herself in the third person throughout shows us that she is contemplating the possibility of a relationship with Odysseus, even though she does not yet even know his name. Nausicaa is attracted to Odysseus. However, unlike Calypso, she does not attempt to act on her attraction; in this she is still strongly aware of propriety and proper actions in her society.

Task: Comparing Calypso and Nausicaa

Compare and contrast the characters and roles of Calypso in Book Five with Nausicaa in Book Six.

- Read Books five and Six again.
- Make a bullet point list on the similarities and differences between these two characters.
- In what ways has Homer developed these characters?

Comparing Nausicaa and Calypso

Nausicaa and Calypso are two very different women and have different roles to play in the *Odyssey*. Their different approaches to *xenia* differentiate them. Whereas Nausicaa is a role-model of positive *xenia*, Calypso's *xenia* is somewhat less than ideal.

Nausicaa is a princess of a polite and cultured people. She has practiced the social code since her birth. She treats Odysseus, despite his circumstances with care. She invites him to her father's palace, just as would be expected of a host to a supplicant guest.

In stark comparison, Calypso abuses her guest. Although she does not mistreat Odysseus in that she provides shelter, warmth and food (even becoming Odysseus' lover), she has imprisoned Odysseus against his wishes, despite his desire to depart, it is she that prevents him from doing so.

The two women differ in other ways; Calypso is an immortal goddess, a divine who is confident and open about her sexuality. For her, the rules of human social behaviour do not apply, if she chooses otherwise; whereas Nausicaa, being a mortal woman of noble birth, cannot be seen openly in the company of a man without potential damage to her reputation. Calypso, on the other hand,   lives outside human society by virtue of being a goddess, and the rules of decent human behaviour do not matter.

As an unmarried young woman, Nausicaa is far less sure of herself than is Calypso, and is certainly not free to take lovers as Calypso has done. However, whilst Calypso is confident in her divinity and immortality; Nausicaa is much more of an innocent; a young princess who still enjoys such child-like pursuits as playing catch on the beach.

There is some humour in the scene of the emergence of the rather naked and sea-torn Odysseus into the presence of Nauiscaa and her entourage. Nausicaa's maids run screaming in fear at the sight of this grimy man whose only clothes are a 'leafy bough' he is holding to conceal himself. Nausicaa, in contrast, stands her ground. She is a princess, and unlike her maids, her duty as an aristocrat is to swallow her fear and greet the stranger as courtesy and *xenia* require.

It is Nausicaa's offer of *xenia* to Odysseus that is crucial in Odysseus achieving his *'Nostos'* or homecoming.

Task: An examination style commentary question

Reread the passage Book VI.273-288

> *'Now it is their unpleasant gossip that I wish to avoid. .. before being properly married'.*

How successfully does Homer portray Nausicaa's thoughts and feelings in this passage?

Remember to pay attention both to the language used and the events described

---

3.3 Book Seven: The Phaeacians: Realism and fantasy

In this section we will;

- *Explore and understand the content and style of Book Seven*

- *Consider the role and function of the palace in the Odyssey*

- *Explore the character of the Phaeacian people*

- *Explore the character and personality of Odysseus*

- *Explore some of the descriptive language used by Homer*

Book Seven of the *Odyssey*

This topic will help you to understand the seventh book of the *Odyssey*. In this book Homer examines the Phaeacians in greater detail and how Odysseus interacts with such a generous and kind people. This section examines how Homer portrays the realistic and fantastic elements whilst Odysseus visits the Phaeacians.

Task: Comprehending Book Seven

Read Book Seven of the Odyssey

Once you have, write brief responses to the following questions;

- *How are the Phaeacians portrayed in Book Seven?*
- *How is Odysseus portrayed in Book Seven?*
- *What language does Homer use to describe the palace and people Odysseus encounters?*

Book Seven: Synopsis

In Book Seven, Odysseus enters the city of the Phaeacians and makes his way to the palace. He follows the advice of Nausicaa and appeals for help from Nausicaa's mother Arete.

Characters in Book Seven

The following characters are present in Book Seven of the Odyssey;

- *Odysseus*
- *Nausicaa, a Phaeacian Princess*
- *Eurymedusa, Nausicaa's maid*
- *Athena*
- *Alcinous, the lord of the Phaeacians*
- *Arete, the lady of the Phaeacians*
- *Echeneus, a Phaeacian noble*
- *Pontonous, Alcinous' squire*

The Structure of Book Seven

Book Seven of the *Odyssey* can most easily be divided into the following sections;

- The city of the Phaeacians (lines 1-81)

- The Palace (lines 82-133)

- Odysseus appeals to Arete (lines 134-end)

The city of the Phaeacians (lines 1-81)

Odysseus approaches the city of the Phaeacians and calls to a girl (Athena disguised) for directions to the palace. Athena then supplies Odysseus with the information he needs to identify the palace. She uses her powers to ensure that Odysseus walks through the city undetected by the Phaeacians, and as they walk, Athena tells Odysseus (and his audience) the background and nature of Arete.

The Palace (lines 82-133)

Arriving at the palace, Odysseus marvels at the wondrous sights that he beholds. Homer provides a detailed description of the palace, its scale and its riches. The palace is full of gold and silver and bronze. Sculpture made by Hephaestus the god of craftsmen himself are present. Whilst the Phaeacian chiefs sit in fine chairs, gold statues of youths are used to hold torches to ensure that the palace is full of light.

The courtyard is full of fruit bearing trees and never fail to provide a never ending supply of fruit and many servants are busy performing tasks. The aim of Homer here is to demonstrate the wealth and splendour of these blessed mortals.

Odysseus appeals to Arete (lines 134-end)

The remainder of this short book is dedicated to Odysseus seeking the help of the Phaeacians. Odysseus enters the palace and reaches Arete unnoticed. He immediately asks for help as a supplicant.

His sudden appearance and supplicant come as a shock to the assembled Phaeacians. Whilst Odysseus waits by the fire, the Phaeacians are for a moment speechless.

It is Echeneus, a councillor of Alcinous that speaks first. He urges Alcinous to offer the stranger hospitality. Alcinous then acts as Echeneus suggests and offers Odysseus perfect *xenia*. Odysseus is bathed and offered refreshment. Alcinous then declares that he will help the stranger with transportation, which he offers without knowing anything of his guest; he does however suspect Odysseus of being a god in disguise. Odysseus immediately rejects this and tells Alcinous the truth of his situation. He has arrived in hardship and seeks to return home.

Arete now questions Odysseus. Who is he? Where did he come from? Odysseus replies with part of the truth. He does not reveal who he is – but he informs his audience that he was shipwrecked on the island of Ogygia (the island of Calypso) and had dwelt there for seven years as her prisoner. He was released and sent on his way on a raft. However the God Poseidon shipwrecked him again and it was with difficulty that he was washed up on the island of Scherie.

Odysseus also tells Arete and Alcinous that he asked Nausicaa for help and followed the princess to the city at her suggestion. Alcinous is impressed with his guest – he would welcome him as a son in law, but will gladly offer him xenia until he can help send him on his way.

The Phaeacians

The Phaeacians are the people that are responsible for bringing about Odysseus' *'Nostos,'* or homecoming. The civilisation that is described by Homer comes as a great relief to Odysseus after all his trials and tribulations. Instead of danger and peril Odysseus encounters a warm welcome and safety whilst among the Phaeacians. However, whilst Telemachus discovers hospitality when he visits the historical sites of Sparta and Pylos, Odysseus is guest to a wholly mythical people.

Phaeacia is a fantasy land; and the inhabitants who inhabit it are an isolated group of people. Homer hints at this further with the words he has Alcinous utter;

> *'Nor does it matter if the place is even more remote than Euboea, which is said to be at the world's end by those of our sailors who saw it..'.*
>
> *Book VII.320*

Realism and fantasy:

The Phaeacians

Read the passage Book VII.103-132;

From; *'The house keeps fifty maids employed.'* **To** *'Such were the glorious gifts the gods had bestowed on Alcinous' home'.*

How does Homer convey the lifestyle enjoyed by the Phaeacians?

Make a list of some aspects of the benefits bestowed upon the Phaeacians.

Euboea is one of the largest of the Greek islands and compared to Ithaca is much larger. Euboea is so close to the mainland of Greece that it is now connected by several bridges. Homer is making a point to his audience here; for the Phaeacians, Euboea is the furthest place they can imagine, way out to the west. It is a measure of their distance from the real Greek world that they can't conceive of a land beyond this island.

Life and society among the Phaeacians

In Book Seven of the *Odyssey* there are several vivid descriptions of the Phaeacians and where they live. The impression given is that the Phaeacians are a people living a blessed life; isolated from the toils and dangers associated with war and want, the Phaeacians are exceptionally favoured by the gods, the have been given supernatural skills by them, and they live in a land which is eternally fruitful and fertile.

This passage above is particularly full of details which demonstrate the ease and leisure with which the Phaeacians enjoy. In particular, they are endowed with God-given prowess in both sailing and weaving, for example;

Athena has given them outstanding skill in beautiful crafts and such fine intelligence

Book VII.110

also;

'Their fruit never fails nor runs short, winter or summer alike'

Book VII.117

Not only are the Phaeacians themselves blessed by the gods, but also the land they live in is similarly blessed. Their home has been given an astounding bounty, such that they live in a perpetual harvest time, and never fear the winter. This situation must have been almost an ideal for Homer's audience. In the ancient world Greece was known for the poverty of her soil and the limited farm land available to each city state, which resulted in countless wars and disputes between cities and neighbours.

Clearly, the Phaeacians are specially blessed; and they are crucial in returning Odysseus back to Ithaca after all his trials and tribulations.

Odysseus and the Phaeacians

Odysseus has Nausicaa to thank for leading him to the palace of Alcinous and his wife Arete, a place of wealth and splendour. However, the purpose of the Phaeacians in the story is not merely to provide shelter for Odysseus before he continues on with his journey, Odysseus needs to see what it is to be among people again and to understand what it is to have honour and reputation once more.

When Homer first introduced Odysseus in Book 5, he was a broken man, wearied after many years and completely alone, aside from the Goddess Calypso on her island of Ogygia. Poseidon's continued rage has prevented Odysseus from making it home to Ithaca.

Without the intervention of the other gods, Athena in particular, Odysseus is forever condemned to be marooned with Calypso and never able to escape back to the reality of Ithaca. Odysseus is finally helpless at this point, for all his strength and endurance. It the Phaeacians who provide Odysseus with the means for returning home.

In Book 7 Alcinous constantly reassures Odysseus that he will get home. Alcinous demonstrates what could be called a perfect *xenia*, unlike Calypso who is in direct contrast to him, indeed; Alcinous is at pains to reassure Odysseus' that he will get safe passage home.

'But not one of us Phaeacians shall detain you. God forbid such a thing! And to set your mind at rest, I now appoint a day for your departure home: tomorrow.'

Book VII.316-7

Despite their differences, the Phaeacians are recognisably 'Greek', with close resemblance to the societies that Homer reveals at Sparta, Pylos as well as at Ithaca. Like the Greeks, the Phaeacians recognise the code of *xenia* which binds all kinds of society and peoples in Homer's world together. What is portrayed by the Phaeacians then is an 'idealised' version of the societies that first heard the *Odyssey* performed.

The Gods, the Phaeacians and the *'Nostos'* of Odysseus

Since the Greek conception of their deities was particularly anthropomorphic, the gods often act as if they were human beings. The Gods suffer from all too human emotions, they feel jealous, they desire, they are angered when another god gets the better of them, and worst of all, they cannot stand losing face in front of others; mortal and immortal.

Athena, as the niece of Poseidon, must walk a path between helping Odysseus on the one hand with averting her uncle's hatred of Odysseus. For her to directly aid Odysseus to get home (by herself taking him back there) would no doubt anger Poseidon beyond measure; more importantly, if Athena were to do this, Homer would not had such a story to tell!

As it is, Athena guides Odysseus to the island of the Phaeacians, and lets them do the rest, in the full knowledge that they will then incur the wrath of the Sea God. This clever plot device of Homer's allows the Olympians to stay true to their human emotions, jealousies and internal power struggles.

3.4 Book Eight: *Xenia* and the Heroic Code

In this section we will;

- *Explore and understand the content and style of Book Eight*

- *Consider the role and function of xenia in the Odyssey*

- *Continue to explore the character of the Phaeacian people*

- *Continue to explore the character and personality of Odysseus*

- *Explore the role of story-telling in the Odyssey*

- *Identify and explore the stylistic techniques used by Homer*

Book Eight of the *Odyssey*

This topic will help you to understand the eighth book of the *Odyssey*. Book Eight is a long book; approximately 600 lines long and contains several distinct episodes.

In this book Homer continues to explore the character of the Phaeacians in greater detail and also how Odysseus interacts with this generous and kind people. This section examines how Homer portrays the heroic code of *timé* and *kleos*.

Task: Comprehending Book Eight

Read Book Eight of the Odyssey

Once you have, write brief responses to the following questions;

- *How are the Phaeacians presented in Book Eight?*
- *How is Odysseus portrayed in Book Eight?*
- *Think about the themes of timé and kleos. How important are these themes in this part of the Odyssey?*

Book Eight: Synopsis

In Book Eight Odysseus is entertained by his hosts whilst the ship is being prepared the Phaeacians demonstrate their prowess in a variety of sporting activities. Athena continues to work for Odysseus behind the scenes, she covers Odysseus in a glamour, that makes him appear godlike.

One Phaeacian, named Eurylaus, is not impressed he taunts Odysseus, who angered, throws a discus far beyond what the others are capable of. The Phaeacians return to the palace for a feast and listen to stories of the Trojan War. These tales cause Odysseus grief and at the pressing of Alcinous, Odysseus agrees to tell the story of his travels.

Another prominent character in Book Eight is the bard Demodocus. He sings a variety of poems about the Trojan War (the fame of this event has even reached the Phaeacians on their distant island). These stories however are source of both pride and grief for Odysseus; on the one hand, he is reminded of his own former fame and prowess and on the other, he is lamenting the loss of his comrades. At the end of Book Eight, Odysseus is appealed upon by his hosts to reveal something of his background and the stage is set for Odysseus to tell the story of his *Odyssey*.

Characters in Book Eight

The following characters are present in Book Eight of the Odyssey;

- *Odysseus*
- *Athena*
- *Alcinous, the lord of the Phaeacians*
- *Arete, the lady of the Phaeacians*
- *Laodamas, the son of Alcinous and Arete*
- *Nausicaa, the Phaeacian princess*
- *Eurylaus, a Phaeacian noble*
- *Demodocus, the court bard*

The Structure of Book Eight

Book Eight of the *Odyssey* can most easily be divided into the following sections;

- *The Phaeacians feast (lines 1-96)*

- *The Games (lines 97-249)*

- *The story of Hephaestus, Aphrodite and Ares (lines 250-366)*

- *The xenia of the Phaeacians (lines 367-468)*

- *Odysseus and Demodocus (lines 469-end)*

The Phaeacians feast (lines 1-96)

Book Eight commences with the Goddess Athena rousing the Phaeacians and encouraging them to attend the assembly where they can witness the stranger now amongst them. She encourages them by stating that this guest is like an 'immortal god'. This is intentional. Odysseus then is to be seen by the Phaeacians as a man with a heroic visage. He does not disappoint. When Odysseus is brought before the assembly; he is covered in a glamour that makes him appear all the more impressive. All of this helps with Odysseus' *kleos*. He is impressive and as a result has some good standing among his hosts, but as yet they are not aware of his *timé*. Homer specifically states that Athena does this so that;

> *'Athene invested his head and shoulders with a divine beauty, and made him seem taller and broader, so that he would inspire the whole Phaeacian people not only with affection but with fear and respect, and might emerge successfully from the many tests they later subjected him to.'*
>
> *Book VIII.19-23*

Alcinous orders a ship to be prepared to speed Odysseus on his way, and also a feast to entertain his guest. This feast is a sacrifice, with many animals killed in order to feed a large number of people.

It is from lines 61-80 in book eight that the bard Demodocus is introduced and described. It is from this description that many Ancient Greeks thought they saw a description of Homer himself. Demodocus is blind and tells the story of an argument between Odysseus and Achilles before Troy. This tale upsets Odysseus and his grief is noticed by Alcinous. This is the first of three stories that Demodocus tells us of in book eight.

The Phaeacian bard Demodocus reminds us of the hero Odysseus and his feats at Troy (although how exactly he might have got news of these events is nicely overlooked by Homer). Also in Book Eight, reveals his heroic status in preparation for announcing his true identity, which he does at the beginning of Book Nine.

The Games (lines 97-249)

Alcinous is a graceful host. He notices Odysseus' grief at the tale of Demodocus, but he does not draw attention to it. Instead Alcinous orders that the Phaeacians compete in a series of games. In lines 110-120, Homer names some of the competing Phaeacians; their names are nautical puns and Homer and successive poets who performed this tale in the Ancient World may have simply made these names up on the spot in order to entertain his audience.

Alcinous' son Laodamas is curious about the prowess of Odysseus. Surely he would like to take part? A Phaeacian names Eurylaus encourages Laodamas and Odysseus is approached. Odysseus however is reluctant to take part. He is here to seek help, not to show off his talents. Eurylaus mistakes Odysseus' reluctance to take part in the games as a weakness, likening him to a merchant captain (lines 159-164). In response to this Odysseus replies in anger and decides to demonstrate to the Phaeacians what he can do. He flings a discus far beyond what his hosts could do. Odysseus has protected his *timé* and enhanced with this action his *kleos.*

Odysseus now offers to take on the Phaeacians in any competition they care to challenge him in; the only one he admits he might struggle with is running; he is after all not the youngest anymore. Odysseus also reveals to the Phaeacians something of his story; he was indeed a participant in the Trojan War, and a prominent one also.

Odysseus does not suffer fools gladly, and when he comes across such a character, like Eurylaus, his response is harsh. Odysseus knows that a man such as Eurylaus is inferior to himself in most if not all deeds and actions, and he does not allow this kind of character to remain ignorant of his own inferiority. Eurylaus however makes amends later in the book with an apology and the gift of a fine sword. Odysseus in turn demonstrates acceptance of this gift and the reconciliation is completed.

The story of Hephaestus, Aphrodite and Ares (lines 250-366)

Odysseus has impressed his hosts and the competitive games cease. No-one cares to challenge Odysseus, but Alcinous, though he admits that Odysseus could best the Phaeacians in any number of sports, does try to rebalance the situation by demonstrating the dancing skills of the Phaeacians.

Now it is Odysseus' turn to be impressed. As the dancers dance, the bard Demodocus performs his second story. In this story, Demodocus tells of the adulterous relationships of the Gods; in particular that of Ares and Aphrodite who are trapped by the cunning of Hephaestus, the spurned husband of Aphrodite. The master craftsman outwits the god of war and Ares and Aphrodite are snared in the act of lovemaking in a cunning net attached to Hephaestus' bed.

The other gods gather around and make fun of how Ares has been caught by the lame god Hephaestus. Only when the God Poseidon offers to act as a guarantor that compensation will be paid is Ares released.

The *xenia* of the Phaeacians (lines 367-468)

The dancing continues with the deployment of a ball that mirrors the playing of Nausicaa and her maids in Book Six. Odysseus complements this dancing and this praise is gratefully received by Alcinous. The Phaeacians now present Odysseus with gifts; many of them. A sword is offered by Eurylaus and this gift reconciles him with Odysseus. Odysseus is also granted a talent weight of gold; an immense sum for most Greeks; by the 5th century BC, a talent of gold would pay to maintain a trireme warship and its several hundred crew at sea for around five months of service.

Odysseus is bathed and granted further gifts from Arete and Nausicaa bids Odysseus farewell with kind words. Odysseus relies that he will be forever grateful; it was Nausicaa who gave him back his life (line 468)

Odysseus and Demodocus (lines 469-end)

Another feast is prepared and Odysseus takes pains to offer to the bard a choice cut of meat. The final story told by Demodocus and is a request by Odysseus. He wishes to hear of the fall of Troy and the story of the wooden horse in which he himself plays a prominent role. Odysseus is full of praise of the abilities of Demodocus the bard. Although not a hero, Demodocus commands Odysseus' respect. It is his stories that drive Odysseus to tears on several occasions in Book Eight, something that many of the challenges and dangers faced by Odysseus cannot do.

The perfect *xenia* of Alcinous

At the beginning of Book Eight, Alcinous demonstrates his hospitality and generosity. We have already seen examples of excellent xenia offered to Telemachus by Nestor and Menelaus. Good as their hospitality is. It is exceeded by Alcinous. He does not as yet know who Odysseus his, only that he is a stranger who wants to go home. Alcinous is determined to help Odysseus in this and whilst preparations are being made to ready the ship, Odysseus is to be entertained and he is given a fortune in gifts.

When Odysseus is upset by Demodocus' tale, it is Alcinous who notices Odysseus' distress. But rather than shame his guest by drawing attention to his grief, Alcinous instead suggests that Demodocus should cease his story and that games be held. Later on, when Demodocus' tale of the fall of Troy once again drives Odysseus to tears, Alcinous once again asks the bard to cease his storytelling without drawing attention to Odysseus' distress and knowing that Odysseus is in some way connected with Troy asks Odysseus to reveal his identity. This shows Alcinous' fine demonstration of *xenia* and his sensitivity to the needs of his guest.

Task: Odysseus in Book Eight, lines 521-545

Read this passage;

'While the famous minstrel was singing, Odysseus' heart was melting with grief. .. to any man with the slightest common sense, a guest and suppliant is as close as a brother.'

How effectively does Homer portray Odysseus in this passage?

Odysseus' character as seen among the Phaeacians

In the earlier Books Six and Seven, Odysseus demonstrates his grace and charm when he first meets Nausicaa. He goes out of his way to ensure that he would be well-received by her. In Book Eight Odysseus shows proper respect towards his hosts and polite Phaeacians but other Phaeacians that seek to abuse Odysseus because of his situation are challenged by the hero.

Odysseus' character is certainly multi-faceted. Indeed, Homer makes great effort to portray Odysseus as a fully fleshed out individual, with both good and bad sides on display to the audience. This makes Odysseus all the more believable.

Task: Odysseus and the Phaeacians

'The Phaeacians are the saviours of Odysseus, rather than the gods, including Athena'.

How far do you agree with this statement?

Odysseus in Book Eight lines 521-545

This section of Book Eight includes a poignant description of Odysseus at this point in the *Odyssey*. Odysseus' heart is described as 'melting'; a vivid metaphor. In his grief Odysseus heart is turning into water, and implies that our hero is consumed by grief.

Then follows a Homeric simile;

'He wept as a woman weeps when she throws her arms around the body of her beloved husband, fallen in battle in the defence of his city and his comrades, fighting to save his city and his children from the evil day .'

Book VIII.522-525

This is a very appropriate simile for Homer to use here; not only does it provide a apt description of how the women of Troy might have felt when their city fell to the Greeks, It also apt because Odysseus, as a leading participant in the Trojan war, was very much responsible for the destruction of the city and the grief of the women of Troy.

Odysseus is alone in his grief, and is overwhelmed by the story told by Demodocus. In contrast the Phaeacians have had no experience of the war like Odysseus has had, and so they cannot understand his personal anguish either.

Finally for Odysseus to be likened to a woman in the first place is highly unusual for a Greek hero in play or poem. When a hero is likened to a woman in such circumstances it is used to imply that they are cowardly or otherwise unmanly. In this particular case though, the simile here is not to portray Odysseus as cowardly, it is to make the audience feel great sympathy for Odysseus.

Odysseus is revealed

It is only now that Alcinous asks who Odysseus is. This is necessary plot wise, as Alcinous needs to know which island to take Odysseus to. Alcinous also reveals that there is a prophecy that would one day see a sentient Phaeacian ship wrecked and mountains thrown up around their island, land-locking the city. Who then is the man who is Alcinous' guest?

Part Four: The *Odyssey*

Part Four: The *Odyssey*

4.1 Book Nine: The Cyclops

4.2 Book Ten: Circe

4.3 Book Eleven: Odysseus in the Underworld

4.4 Book Twelve: The Cattle of the Sun

The Odyssey

Odysseus now announces his identity and begins to tell the story of his journey from Troy. Odysseus and his Ithacans set sail from Troy in twelve ships. Making landfall, the Ithacans plunder a city of the Cicones. The Ithacans have some success but are then driven into the sea by reinforcements. Sailing away they are hit by a storm as they sail south of the Peloponnese and are driven by the storm winds to the land of the Lotus eaters.

Escaping the temptations of this land, Odysseus leads his fleet to the land of the Cyclops, where he lands with a small scouting party and makes his way to the cave of the Cyclops Polyphemus. Polyphemus rejects the traditional offer of hospitality and imprisons Odysseus and his companions and begins to eat them.

Odysseus and his men are trapped in the cave and in order to escape Odysseus gets Polyphemus drunk and then blinds him with a sharpened stake. They escape from the cave by hiding under the fleeces of Polyphemus' sheep and set sail. As the Ithacans sail away however, Odysseus shouts out his name to boast to Polyphemus. The cyclops retaliates by praying to his father Poseidon to avenge his son's blindness.

Continuing their journey, the Ithacans reach the island of Aeolus, the god of the winds. He entertains Odysseus and his men and sets them on their way with a bag that contains all contrary winds. However, as the Ithacan fleet reaches sight of their home, Odysseus' crew open the bag and release the winds. The fleet is driven back to the island of Aeolus, who now sees that the Ithacans are under some kind of curse. He refuses to help them.

Setting sail again the Ithacans reach the land of the cannibal Laestrygonians. Here Odysseus loses all of his men, aside from his own ship. With this single ship Odysseus sails on and reaches the island of Circe. This goddesses at first greets the Ithacans with sorcery; transforming many of his men into pigs. Odysseus goes to confront Circe and is helped by Hermes who gives him a plant that repels Circes' magic. Circe then becomes much more welcoming, returning his men to their former selves and hosting them for a year.

Odysseus however still yearns for Ithaca and is told by Circe to seek the knowledge of the dead prophet Teiresias. Odysseus sails to the gateway of the Underworld and speaks to a parade of the illustrious dead. Teiresias tells Odysseus how to get home; he will face perils, but so long as he and his men do not eat the cattle of Hyperion all will be well.

Odysseus returns to Circe's island and bids her and a dead crewman farewell. Odysseus avoids the perils of the Siren song and escapes the whirlpool of Charybdis by losing a few men to the monster Scylla, but on reaching the island of the Sun God they are marooned there by contrary winds. At last hungry the Ithacans kill and eat some of Hyperion's cattle while they wait for the wind to change.

Setting sail at last, Hyperion threatens to take the sun to the Underworld if Zeus refuses to punish the Ithacans. Zeus strikes Odysseus' ship with a thunderbolt, destroying it and killing all of the Ithacans. Only Odysseus survives and he is washed up on the island of Ogygia where he spends the next seven years as a guest of Calypso.

4.1 Book Nine: The Cyclops

In this section we will;

- *Explore and understand the content and style of Book Nine*

- *Consider the role and function of xenia in the Odyssey*

- *Continue to explore the character of the Cyclops*

- *Continue to explore the character and personality of Odysseus*

- *Explore the role of story-telling in the Odyssey*

- *Identify and explore the stylistic techniques used by Homer*

- *Examine the theme of story-telling in the Odyssey*

- *Consider the presentation of monsters*

- *Consider the theme of disguise and recognition*

Book Nine of the *Odyssey*

Books Nine to Twelve of the Odyssey are the most famous parts of the Odyssey. In these books they recount the tale of Odysseus' journey from Troy to his shipwreck on Calypso's island.

In this section examines the theme of story-telling, disguise and the role of monsters in the *Odyssey*. In particular, this section explores one of the most well-known episodes of Homer's *Odyssey*, the encounter with the monstrous Cyclops, Polyphemus.

Task: Comprehending Book Nine

Read Book Nine of the Odyssey

Once you have, write brief responses to the following questions;

- *How the people that Odysseus encounters are presented in Book Nine?*
- *How is Odysseus portrayed in Book Nine?*
- *What stylistic and linguistic techniques are used by Homer in Book Nine?*
- *How effective are they?*

Book Nine synopsis

Odysseus now announces his identity and begins to tell the story of his journey from Troy. Odysseus and his Ithacans set sail from Troy in twelve ships.

Making landfall, the Ithacans plunder a city of the Cicones. The Ithacans have some success but are then driven into the sea by reinforcements. Sailing away they are hit by a storm as they sail south of the Peloponnese and are driven by the storm winds to the land of the Lotus eaters.

Escaping the temptations of this land, Odysseus leads his fleet to the land of the Cyclops, where he lands with a small scouting party and makes his way to the cave of the Cyclops Polyphemus. Polyphemus rejects the traditional offer of hospitality and imprisons Odysseus and his companions and begins to eat them.

Odysseus and his men are trapped in the cave and in order to escape Odysseus gets Polyphemus drunk and then blinds him with a sharpened stake. They escape from the cave by hiding under the fleeces of Polyphemus' sheep and set sail. As the Ithacans sail away however, Odysseus shouts out his name to boast to Polyphemus. The cyclops retaliates by praying to his father Poseidon to avenge his son's blindness.

Characters in Book Nine

The following characters are present in Book Nine of the Odyssey;

- *Odysseus*
- *Ithacans*
- *Cicones*
- *Lotus Eaters*
- *Polyphemus*

The Structure of Book Nine

- *An Introduction (lines 1-38)*

- *The Cicones Episode (lines 39-82)*

- *The Lotus Eaters (lines 83-104)*

- *Description of the land of the Cyclops (lines 105-169)*

- *Polyphemus (lines 170-end)*

An Introduction (lines 1-38)

These lines of Book Nine are an introduction. Odysseus reveals his true identity. On several occasions previously, Odysseus claims that the Gods have inflicted misfortune on him – but we must question as we read the following important point. Do the actions of Odysseus and his Ithacans justify the wrath of the Gods?

The Cicones Episode (lines 39-82)

Odysseus recounts how he and his men attack the city of Ismarus; which is inhabited by people known as Cicones. Ismarus is sacked; the men are killed and the women and the property are plundered and divided up among the Ithacans. However, Odysseus' men ignore his orders to leave as soon as they have gathered all the plunder.

Instead the Ithacans remain in the area to enjoy their spoils of war. This is a mistake. The Cicones from other cities arrive and attack, defeating the Ithacans in battle. From each of the twelve ships, six men are killed in this fight.

Further misfortune follows. As the ships sail away, they are struck by a storm which drives them past Cape Malea and the island of Cythera. These geographical locations in the southern Peloponnese and just off its coast are the last identifiable locations in Books Nine through Twelve. From this point forward, Homer has Odysseus in the mythical world.

After ten days of being driven by the storm the Ithacans arrive in the land of the lotus eaters.

The Lotus Eaters (lines 83-104)

As the fleet makes landfall, Odysseus sends a three man scouting party out to investigate the land. These three Ithacans meet the Lotus Eaters and consume the lotus fruit. This mythical fruit makes the Ithacans blissfully happy and they decide to remain among the lotus people and do nothing other than eat this addictive fruit. Odysseus however discovers what has befallen his men and has to drag them back to the ships by force rather than permit his other men to surrender to this temptation. The Ithacans set sail.

Description of the land of the Cyclops (lines 105-169)

This part of Book Nine begins with a description of the Cyclops country. The picture of both land and its inhabitants are wild and uncivilised – they know no laws, no assemblies and possess no interest in their neighbours and they possess no ships.

Odysseus also describes that close by is a 'luxuriant island'; a perfect place to live and also a great place to harbour ships at. The Ithacans land on this island in a fog that causes their ships to ground; but without damage. The Ithacans encounter many goats and eat well, drinking wine they seized from the Cicones. As the sun sets the Ithacans see smoke made by the inhabitants and hear the bleats of the sheep and goats that graze in the land of the Cyclops.

Polyphemus (lines 170-end)

> *"whether they are aggressive savages with no sense of right or wrong or hospitable and god-fearing people".*
>
> *Book IX.173-175*

In the remainder of Book Nine, Homer recounts the episode of Odysseus and the Cyclops Polyphemus. Odysseus takes his ship over to the land of the Cyclops in order to investigate whether the Cyclops are savage or hospitable. Taking a party of a dozen men with him, Odysseus soon discovers an inhabited cave. With him Odysseus takes a gift of vintage wine given to him by Maron, a priest of Apollo whom Odysseus spared when he sacked Ismarus. Homer then briefly digresses on this wine and other treasure obtained (lines 195-211).

Homer then has Odysseus describe the cave. It is full of cheese and young sheep and goats in pens as well as pottery. Odysseus' men suggest that they take what they want and leave whilst the homeowner is away. Odysseus refuses (something he and his men will regret).

Presently the Cyclops arrives with his herd. As he enters he blocks the cave with a boulder, milks his ewes and lights a fire. He then notices his 'guests'.

A brief exchange occurs between Odysseus and the Cyclops (lines 250-286). His first words include '*Stranger*' which compares with Nestors first words to Telemachus in Book Three (lines 71-75). The wording is almost identical – however what follows is very different.

The Cyclops demands to know about the strangers. Pretending that he has been shipwrecked, Odysseus appeals for hospitality; the laws of Zeus protect those in need. In response to this, Polyphemus is dismissive, showing that the laws of the Gods are an irrelevance to him. He asks of Odysseus' ship, on being told by Odysseus that they are shipwrecked, the Cyclops retorts by consuming two of Odysseus' men for dinner. He does this with the assistance of a simile '*like a mountain lion*'. After his meal, he sleeps.

Remember!

'Achaeans' is another word that Homer uses to describe the Greeks.

Despite his obvious fear of the Cyclops, Odysseus' speech is a model of careful and artful persuasion. For example, he starts by introducing himself and his men as 'Achaeans' and, that they are survivors of the Trojan War.

No doubt, this is done in an attempt to inspire the Cyclops to show due respect and honour. Odysseus continues by referring to the sacking of Troy. He does this in order to give the impression to the Cyclops that he is a warrior and a brave man. This might work on the Phaeacians, but the Cyclops is either ignorant of, or unheeding of, this great event of men.

Odysseus then appeals to the Polyphemus' pity and sense of hospitality, they are 'suppliants' and should be treated with respect and assistance. Odysseus finishes by reminding Polyphemus that *xenia* is sacred to Zeus himself, and that not only *should* he help out of pity and decency, but he also has a religious duty to do so.

The Cyclops again is dismissive of this attempt. He is a Cyclops and he does what he wants. The Cyclops is uninterested in the deeds of men, and because the Cyclops is not human, he is immune to arguments of pity. He has none for the men in his cave, who he instead sees only as entertainment and a meal. The Cyclops also has no fear or respect for the gods, even Zeus. Polyphemus' response to Odysseus clearly demonstrates that he is a monster.

A bust depicting Polyphemus

However, the Cyclops is not a straightforward monster;

- *Polyphemus can speak, think and reason.*

- *Polyphemus keeps sheep and goats, with his love for his animals clear both before and after his blinding.*

- *Polyphemus has a home. His cave seems to have many features of a rural house: he stores cheeses, and brings firewood to cook, warm and light his home.*

- *He is anthropomorphic; though a giant, he is clearly imagined as human in form.*

Odysseus evolves a plan to deal with the Cyclops and also to escape. He spots in the cave a green olive wood staff – more like a ship's mast (incidentally an olive branch was used by Greek heralds as a symbol to indicate that they wanted to organise truces and peace treaties – Odysseus puts his olive branch to a very different use!). This staff is made into a spear.

With the assistance of two men he will spear the Cyclops in the eye whilst he sleeps. When the Cyclops returns after a day of shepherding he eats two more men and then settles in for the evening. Odysseus offers the Cyclops some of his vintage wine. Polyphemus accepts and asks Odysseus his name. Odysseus replies that his name is 'Nobody'.

Ou tis/ me tis/ metis – a Greek pun

In this famous incident Odysseus tricks the Cyclops by calling himself 'Nobody'.

The Greek for *'nobody'* is *'ou tis'*; whilst the Greek for *'no-one'* is *'me tis'*.

An Ancient Greek audience would not fail to notice that 'me tis' sounds the same as *'metis'* which is the Greek word for 'cunning' or 'resourcefulness'; the very word often used to define Odysseus.

As the Cyclops sleeps in a drunken stupor, vomiting in his sleep as he does so, Odysseus acts. Taking his olive wood spear he drives it into the eye of Polyphemus. Homer uses several similes to describe this action (lines 381-389) and the subsequent destruction of the eye (lines 390-393).

Other Cyclopes hear the cries of Polyphemus and investigate. But they can make no sense from him. Polyphemus seems insane – nobody has blinded him. The other cyclopes depart presuming that Polyphemus is mentally unwell; an affliction caused by the gods.

Odysseus and his men escape when Polyphemus opens his cave to let his flock out. They hide under the bellies of the rams and once they have escaped Odysseus and his surviving men steal the flock and set sail.

Polyphemus wanders blindly out of his cave and hears the departure of Odysseus' ship. Odysseus taunts the blinded monster and receives in return a boulder thrown in the direction of his voice. Ignoring the advice of his crew, Odysseus taunts Polyphemus again and reveals his name.

Polyphemus recalls it is his fate to be blinded by a man named Odysseus and calls on his father Poseidon to punish Odysseus. Let him never return home. But if he is fated to reach home, let him do so late, alone, and in a foreign ship and when he is home let him face trouble there also.

Task: Polyphemus

Consider the Cyclops episode of Book Nine.

Points to consider could include;

- Do you think it is possible to sympathise with the Cyclops?
- How does he view Odysseus and his comrades?
- How well does the Cyclops use *xenia*?

The theme of recognition in the *Odyssey* at the beginning of Book Nine

Like in any good poem or story, the books of the *Odyssey* flow seamlessly from one to the other. Returning briefly to Book Eight, Alcinous asks his mysterious guest to reveal his name and his past. Alcinous has been told little by Odysseus, other than he is a veteran of the Trojan War who has been shipwrecked and that Demodocus' story of the Trojan War has caused him grief.

In much the same way that Telemachus has journeyed to visit his father's old friends and comrades; Nestor and Menelaus, and this has served to establish Telemachus' identity as his father's son and his future role as the rightful heir of Odysseus. Likewise, this episode of introduction serves to establish Odysseus' identity as one of the great heroes of the Trojan War.

Structure and Story-telling in the *Odyssey.*

Story-telling is all-important in the *Odyssey*. The power of the bard Demodocus in Book Eight has already amply demonstrated this importance. In Books Nine through Twelve there is a shift of emphasis; this is *Odysseus'* story and it is he, Odysseus, who tells the tale.

We have had Books One to Four, are often called the *Telemachy*, because they establish the role and character to Telemachus. Books Five to Eight have been told by Homer, often in the third person of how Odysseus arrives among the Phaeacians.

Now in Books Nine to Twelve, the story of the *Odyssey* shifts to Odysseus' earlier adventures and it is Odysseus himself who takes up the tale. This plotting technique, of telling the story out of chronological order, adds variety and depth to the poem.

The Cyclops and *Xenia.*

One of the major themes of the *Odyssey* reoccurs in this episode, *xenia*. Throughout the *Odyssey*, different characters use or abuse *xenia*. On the one hand, it is possible for immortal goddesses such as Calypso, to abuse *xenia* since they do not have to abide by rules in the same ways as human beings. Likewise, it is possible for a one-eyed giant to abuse *xenia* since he occupies a grey area between human and monster.

Polyphemus demonstrates his civilised nature through his powers of speech and his demonstration of human like characteristics discussed above, but he also demonstrates his monstrous savagery. These acts are also gross abuses of *xenia*. For example, he;

- *Polyphemus is rude from the outset.*

- *Polyphemus does not automatically extend courtesy, welcome and greeting to Odysseus and his companions.*

- *Polyphemus offers no guest-gifts, though he is willing to accept that of the wine from Odysseus.*

- *Polyphemus eats his guests and he eats them raw. This is a key indicator of his status as a 'monster'.*

The cunning of Odysseus

Thinking back to Book One, In the first line of the *proem of the Odyssey,* Odysseus is described as resourceful. Indeed, Odysseus' character is defined by his 'resourcefulness' or cunning. In the Cyclops episode Odysseus is portrayed as both cunning and deceptive. First of all he determines that although he could kill Polyphemus as he sleeps, he and his men could not escape the cave. Polyphemus needs to be tricked into letting them escape the cave by removing the stone that blocks the way out.

The Cyclops episode is possibly the most famous and notable example of this cunning at work. Odysseus' crafty plot is to befuddle the Cyclops with the strong wine he brought from the ship, then to blind the Cyclops. Forced to let his herd of sheep out to

pasture the Cyclops opened the cave and groped and grasped to prevent the men from escaping. However, once again, Odysseus out thinks Polyphemus and Odysseus and his men escape from the cave by hiding underneath the sheep.

There is much *pathos,* or sympathy generated in the description of the Cyclops' blinding. Although a monster, Polyphemus cares for his animals, and this blinding is detrimental to his ability to carry out his shepherding duties. He is forced to feel for his sheep and goats as they leave the cave and can no longer watch them closely as a good shepherd is accustomed to do.

'No-body'

However, the key manifestation of Odysseus' cunning is demonstrated by refusing to give his name to the Cyclops. Calling himself 'no-body', this verbal trick (actually a pun in Greek) is designed to prevent the Cyclops from getting any help from his fellows after his blinding. The neighbours of Polyphemus come to help him, but his cries that 'nobody' is hurting him send them away again.

It is Odysseus' ability to trick and outwit those he meets, and also to disguise himself when the need arrives is perhaps the main skill of Odysseus. He has already 'disguised' himself in the company of the Phaeacians, in so far as he did not reveal his identity to them until he was sure of their behaviour and that they would believe his claims, later on, Odysseus manages to trap the Suitors through use of his disguise as a beggar.

The measure of the importance of disguise as a weapon in the arsenal of Odysseus is his most useful skill. This becomes apparent when, in his pride, Odysseus lets that disguise slip. By revealing his true identity to Polyphemus in an outburst of uncontrolled pride and arrogance, Odysseus miscalculates. Polyphemus has a powerful ally in the shape of his Father, Poseidon, and hearing of the plight of his son, brings down the full wrath of Poseidon.

It is this uncharacteristic slip that is responsible for Odysseus' later troubles; if only he had kept to his disguise, and kept his mouth shut, Odysseus would not incur the wrath of Poseidon and would not be shipwrecked. Therefore, he would have returned much sooner to Ithaca, and the Suitors would never have seen the opportunity of Odysseus' extended absence.

In short, without this prideful slip of Odysseus, there might have been no *Odyssey*. And yet, it is inevitable that Odysseus would boast. He is a hero and a hero who has outwitted and defeated a monster. It is appropriate for an adversary to know who has defeated him in order to secure for the future the hero's *timé* and *kleos.*

Odysseus is fated to blind the Cyclops and reveal his name to Polyphemus. This episode clearly demonstrates the importance to Odysseus of maintaining his disguises, since great tragedy occurs as a result of him forgetting his most important and useful skill.

Task: Examination style response

In an examination, you may be expected to write an extended essay on a particular theme of the *Odyssey*. Below is an examination style question

How far do you agree with the following statement?

'The ability to 'play a part' or assume a disguise is Odysseus' most important and useful skill'

Your answer might include discussion of the following episodes:

- Odysseus' disguises when escaping Polyphemus
- Odysseus withholding his real identity from Nausicaa and the Phaeacians.
- Odysseus disguised as a beggar in Ithaca.

Remember to refer beyond the events of Book Nine: this question is a test of your ability to relate episodes, events and characters across the set text books.

It is also important that you come to a **judgement** in your answer. You must avoid simply 'listing' your examples of use of disguise (effective or otherwise).

Remember to say whether or not you think that 'playing a part' *is* Odysseus' most important skill; and if so why or why not.

4.2 Book Ten: Circe

In this section we will;

- *Explore and understand the content and style of Book Ten of the Odyssey*

- *Explore the ways in which Homer uses language to engage the audience*

- *Examine the role of Odysseus*

- *Examine the role of the Ithacans*

- *Consider some of the stylistic and structural techniques used by Homer*

- *Examine the theme of the supernatural in Book Ten*

- *Consider the role of women in the Odyssey as portrayed by Circe*

Book Ten of the *Odyssey*

This section will help you to understand the tenth book of the *Odyssey*. This section focuses on the structure of Books Nine and Ten as well as considering the role of the events described in them. In particular two this section will examine the Aeolus and Laestrygonian episodes of Book 10. This section also focuses on the parallels evident in the *Odyssey* and on the position of women in Homeric society, through the presentation of the character of Circe.

Task: Comprehending Book Ten

Read Book Ten of the Odyssey. Once you have, write brief responses to the following questions;

- *Consider the similarities and differences between the structure and plots of Books Nine and Ten?*
- *What has Homer focussed on in Book Ten?*
- *How is Odysseus portrayed in Book Three?*
- *Consider how the Ithacans impact upon the narrative in Book Ten?*

Book Ten: Synopsis

In Book Ten the Ithacans continue their journey; the Ithacans reach the island of Aeolus, the god of the winds. He entertains Odysseus and his men and sets them on their way with a bag that contains all contrary winds. However, as the Ithacan fleet reaches sight of their home, Odysseus' crew open the bag and release the winds. The fleet is driven back to the island of Aeolus, who now sees that the Ithacans are under some kind of curse. He refuses to help them.

Setting sail again the Ithacans reach the land of the cannibal Laestrygonians. Here Odysseus loses all of his men, aside from his own ship. With this single ship Odysseus sails on and reaches the island of Circe. This goddesses at first greets the Ithacans with sorcery; transforming many of his men into pigs.

Odysseus goes to confront Circe and is helped by Hermes who gives him a plant that repels Circes' magic. Circe then becomes much more welcoming, returning his men to their former selves and hosting them for a year.

Characters in Book Ten

The following characters are present in Book Ten;

- *Odysseus*
- *Eurylochus, a comrade of Odysseus*
- *Polites, a comrade of Odysseus*
- *Elpenor, an unfortunate Ihacan.*
- *The Ithacans*
- *Aeolus, an immortal*
- *Antiphus, chief of the Laestrygonians*
- *Circe, an immortal*
- *Hermes, the Messenger God*

The Structure of Book Ten

Book Two of the *Odyssey* can most easily be divided into the following sections;

- *The island of Aeolia (lines 1-79)*

- *The Laestrygonians (lines 80-133)*

- *Circe (lines 134-end)*

Task: The bag of winds

Read Book X.27-45 **from**;

'"But his measures were doomed to failure, for we came to grief through our own senseless stupidity. **to**... *Come on; let's find out and see how much gold and silver is hidden in that bag."'*

Using examples from these lines consider how effectively Homer uses language to create tension.

The island of Aeolia (lines 1-79)

In the first episode of Book Ten Odysseus and his crew encounter Aeolus and his family. Aeolus inhabits a floating island and has command of the weather. Favoured of the Gods, Aeolus entertains Odysseus and his men well for a month, another example of the good practice of *xenia*. However, things quickly deteriorate for Odysseus and his crew. Aeolus provides the Ithacans with a bag which contains all the contrary winds; only a gentle west wind is allowed to blow the ships home to Ithaca.

They set sail and Odysseus, fearful of his men's actions, stays awake for nine days. On the last, however, Ithaca comes into sight and Odysseus slumbers. This leads to disaster. Odysseus' men decide to open the bag; thinking it contains treasure. The bag is opened and the ships are driven all the way back to Aeolia. Odysseus appeals to Aeolus to help again. Aeolus refuses, the actions of the Ithacans tells Aeolus that they are cursed by the Gods.

Analysis of lines Book Ten, lines 27-45

First, Homer starts with some gloomy foreshadowing: *'for we came to grief, through our own senseless stupidity'*.

The tension is built up as the audience anticipates what might go wrong for Odysseus and his crew. They have been given a wonderful gift; a bag containing all the winds. This bag, in which the dangerous winds are trapped, will allow Odysseus to return to Ithaca on a calm sea, blown by the gentle west wind that Aeolus has left un-imprisoned.

The tension is further built up by the reference to the length of the journey; all is well for nine days and nights, when Odysseus and his men experience plain sailing, even sighting Ithaca on the tenth day. They are so close to returning home it is even possible to see the fires of home burning (Book 10. Line 30). Then, when their goal is plainly within their grasp, Odysseus, thinking that his journey is over, falls asleep. This error costs him and his men dearly. By surrendering control at this point the crew's curiosity gets the better of them.

A rumour emerges that Odysseus has hidden gold and silver in the bag given him by Aeolus, and they immediately think the worst: that Odysseus is hiding treasure from them, and will not share it (Book 10.line 33-45). The tension is cemented by the final comment;

'Come on; let's find out and see how much gold and silver is hidden in that bag.'

Book X.45

At this point, a moment of calm before the storm, the crew make the decision to doubt Odysseus and reap the consequences of their actions; it is their choice, and it results in their doom.

The Laestrygonians (lines 80-133)

If the *Odyssey* were a historical event that had actually happened, perhaps the most calamitous event for Odysseus' men is the encounter with the Laestrygonians. The Laestrygonian episode is a disaster for Odysseus' men. He is left with a single ship. However, this disaster is mainly a plot device used by Homer.

Odysseus and his fleet arrive at the island of Telepylus, the home of the Laestrygonians. All of Odysseus' ships harbour in a narrow cove, all except Odysseus' ship which he anchors outside the cove. Three men (the same number as are sent in the Lotus Eater episode) are sent to scout out the land. They meet the daughter of Antiphates, chief of the Laestrygonians, and are led to the palace (note the similarities and differences with Book Six and Seven). Here Antiphates kills and eats one of the men. The other two flee and reach Odysseus.

This misfortune is enhanced when the Laestrygonians, who are more like giants than men, throw boulders on the trapped fleet, sinking it and killing the crews. Note the simile of the crew being dragged out of the sea 'like fishes on a spear' (lines 125-6). These men will be eaten later.

The Laestrygonians are a similar race of monster to the Cyclops in so far as they are cannibals, which is in itself an element of repetition by the poet.

Homer introduces them in order that they might get rid of all of Odysseus' ships apart from his own and the few men who are sailing with him. In this, Homer continues the process of whittling down the numbers of Odysseus' men. Some of his men have fallen at the hands of the Cicones and others have been eaten by the Cyclops. Now Odysseus has but one ship and crew. Soon he will not even have these.

Task: The Laestrygonians

Read Book X, lines 80-132

Consider the following;

What do you think the purpose of the Laestrygonian episode is in terms of plot development?

Circe (lines 134-end)

After escaping from the dreaded Laestrygonians, Odysseus and his crew, now in a single ship, arrive at the island of Aeaea. Odysseus goes out scouting and hunting. He discovers a solitary house on the island and determines to send a scouting party to the house to discover something of the inhabitants and also to find out where they are. On his way back the ships he kills a giant stag with his bow, and drags it back to his crew for a meal.

Eurylochus leads a party of twenty-two men to investigate the house and as they approach they hear Circe singing as she weaves. Invited to enter Circe's house, all but Eurylochus accept, and are entertained with a lavish meal, but after being drugged, Circe turns the Ithacans into pigs. Eurylochus then flees back to Odysseus to report the news of this disaster.

Odysseus responds to Eurylochus' story by readying his weapons and heading towards the house of Circe. This bravery demonstrates the difference between a regular mortal man and a hero. On his way to the house, Odysseus encounters the God Hermes who provides Odysseus with the key to defeating Circe's magic; a magic herb named Moly, to protect the hero from the spells of Circe and also instructions on how to defeat Circe. Homer provides his audience with a description of Circe's house (lines 345-375).

The plan works. As they are cured, Homer treats his audience to a nice simile of his Ithacans, bewitched and not, being like a herd of frisky cows (lines 410-418). Odysseus secures the release of his men and the hospitality of her house. In return Circe receives a mortal lover in Odysseus. Once he has been revealed as beloved of the gods, Circe's attitude towards Odysseus and his men changes. Formerly a threat, now she becomes a valued advisor.

Odysseus and his men remain with Circe for a whole year. However, Odysseus still desires to return home to Ithaca. He asks Circe for advice and she instructs him to journey to the Underworld to seek the blind seer Teiresias who can tell him how to get home. However not all of the Ithacans leave the island, Elpenor the youngest and most foolish drinks too much and sleeps on the roof. He falls and is killed.

Task: Charting the *Odyssey*

If you haven't already, read Books Nine and Ten of the *Odyssey*, then complete the following;

- Make a list of the major events that occur in these two books.
- Next, rank these episodes in order of how important you think they are.
- Are there any similarities in the structure of the two books?

The structure of Books Nine and Ten.

Both these books have many structural similarities. Here are the major events of books 9 and 10;

It is noticeable that there are three major events in each of these two books and what is more, these episodes are structured; two shorter incidents precede the climax of the books; the major episode. This structural repetition is yet another example of how the *Odyssey* was composed. However, there is more than this three episode structure that ties the two books together.

Many of the themes we have already discussed find further expression in Book 10, and serve to bind the narrative together further.

Task: Comparing Books Nine and Ten

Read Book Nine lines 88-90 again and then read Book Ten lines 100-102.

Notice the similarities?

This is a short example of repetition of entire sentence chunks or descriptions. Both times, two men are sent with an accompanying herald. Not only are the formulae repeated in the text, but also structures, descriptions and plot formats; in short, Homer is relying on a bank of stock phrases and techniques.

Tensions between Odysseus and his crew

The episode of Aeolus continues a theme that originates from Book 9 lines 40-60; that of the tension between Odysseus and his men. The first example of this tension is within the Cicone's episode: by refusing to leave the city despite Odysseus' instructions they are attacked, and each ship loses six crew members before they escape.

Likewise, in the next episode of Book 9 some of Odysseus' men are intoxicated by the fruit of the lotus, and forget all thoughts of returning home. Again, it is Odysseus who rescues them, since he has always kept his eyes firmly on the goal of reaching Ithaca again. This further identifies him as a hero, in his steadfastness, especially in comparison to his men.

Book Nine

❖ *The attack on the Cicones*

❖ *The Lotus Eaters*

❖ *The Cyclops*

Book Ten

❖ *Aeolus and the bag*

❖ *The Laestrygonians*

❖ *Circe*

Women as drivers of the plot in the *Odyssey*

Unlike in the *Iliad*, where the female characters have a rather limited impact in the development of the plot, in the *Odyssey* it is frequently the female characters who provide the necessary plot devices in order to drive forward the *Odyssey* to its conclusion. The *Odyssey* contains a range of women as plot drivers and also a greater variety and depth of male-female relationships.

For example, the character of Circe is of particular interest. She begins as a threat to Odysseus and his men; however, she quickly becomes a staunch ally of Odysseus and advises him in the next step of his journey.

> **Task: Circe and Calypso**
>
> Compare and contrast the characters of Calypso and Circe.
>
> What similarities and differences are there between the two?
>
> Consider which of these characters is the greater help and the greater hindrance in Odysseus returning home to Ithaca.

Comparing Circe and Calypso

Odysseus has encountered two goddesses who dwell on lonely islands. It is valuable to consider for the moment the similarities and differences between these two goddesses.

❖ **Similarities**

Both female goddesses share much, in that they live on isolated and mysterious islands; both of these locations are products of Homer's imagination. Neither goddess is an Olympian; they also live alone, aside from with their attendants. Both goddesses are also depicted by Homer as having distinctly human characteristics. Both perform human choirs such as weaving and doing other such domestic duties. Both also (to an extent) receive guests with hospitality, as good *xenia* demands.

Both goddesses also live by rules that are different to mortal women, to the extent that they both have a measure of freedom that is denied to mortal women. Whilst mortal women such as

Nausicaa and Penelope live by strict codes of sexual morality, these immortal women live by different rules. Both goddesses also ask for, and receive, a sexual relationship with Odysseus.

❖ **Differences**

Circe, possessing magical powers which she demonstrates beyond those of Calypso, appears to be a greater threat to Odysseus and his men. However, she turns out to be a far more useful ally to Odysseus than Calypso. She gives Odysseus advice to go to the Underworld as well as information on some of the dangers he'll face on the way back to Ithaca.

Unlike Calypso, Circe seems to come across as more removed and distant. She is indifferent to whether or not Odysseus stays or goes. Calypso on the other hand shows some grief at losing Odysseus. It is arguable that Circe is more helpful towards Odysseus, because unlike Calypso, she understands that Odysseus is backed by the gods and confronting her, demonstrates that he is her match.

Whilst Circe is defeated by this combination of Odysseus and the god Hermes, it is Calypso who defeats an Odysseus who is beyond resistance.

Women in the Ancient World

The vast majority of the ancient sources that survive to modern times are written by men. In the ancient sources women are often grouped into two broad categories; those who are obedient to the male orientated society in which they live, and those who are not. These stereotypes are inadequate in fully understanding what life was like for women in Ancient Greece.

Women in ancient Greece generally lacked political rights. They could not attend public assemblies for example. If they were to be associated in any kind of public business, they were required in Athens to have a male relative to speak on their behalf. In Ancient Athens, the most democratic city state, women were discouraged from being seen outside the house if they could manage it.

The role of Mortal Women in the *Odyssey*

Women are crucial to Odysseus getting back to Ithaca. It is his main desire to be reunited with Penelope again that makes him continue on with his journey. Nausicaa is the crucial contact that Odysseus makes that enables his to gain entry to the Phaeacian palace, which eventually gets him back to Ithaca. Arete too is influential in offering Odysseus the hospitality he needs at this point.

Task: Examination style essay response

*How important are Odysseus' relationships with women, mortal **and** immortal?*

Remember to answer the question – don't just give examples of where women are important, but also try to address why it is that they have importance (or not).

You might include discussion of:

- Odysseus' relationship with Nausicaa, Circe, Calypso, Athena and Penelope
- His relationship with any other minor female characters.

The role of Immortal Women in the *Odyssey*

Athena's patronage of Odysseus is vital to Odysseus' safety, and she also keeps watch over his son Telemachus. Circe also makes an important impression on Odysseus. Although he overcomes Circe, she is still inclined to help him get home.

Calypso gives Odysseus hospitality and shelter but keeps him prisoner on Ogygia. This is important because she Odysseus to reach Ithaca. Although she keeps him prisoner, she demonstrates clearly to the audience of the potential power that female characters have in the *Odyssey*.

However, all types of women in the *Odyssey* still remain constrained by the attitudes of the patriarchal society and times in which they live. Nausicaa for example is clearly subject to the wishes of her family.

The subordinate position of women therefore extends even into the realm of the gods, for all her power Athena must be subordinate to the will of Zeus, her father, and the whims of Poseidon, her uncle. Likewise Calypso is eventually controlled by the will of Zeus, which is transmitted through the messenger Hermes.

There is a strong taboo in the *Odyssey* against adultery (where it concerns women anyway); this is important because Penelope is consistently praised because she does not take the far easier option of giving up Odysseus for dead and marrying. The ghost of Agamemnon praises Penelope as the best of wives, in stark contrast to his adulterous and murderous wife Clytemnestra.

4.2 Book Eleven: Odysseus in the Underworld

In this section we will;

- *Explore and understand the content and style of Book Eleven of the Odyssey*

- *Explore the ways in which Homer uses language to engage the audience*

- *Examine the role of the Dead in the Odyssey*

- *Examine the theme of justice and revenge in Book Eleven*

- *Consider some of the stylistic and structural techniques used by Homer*

- *Examine the theme of the supernatural in Book Eleven*

Book Eleven of the *Odyssey*

This section will help you to understand the Eleventh Book of the *Odyssey*. Book Eleven is a departure in style and content from the rest of Homer's works. Odysseus moves from the land of the living to journey to Hades in order to seek advice from the Theban seer Teiresias. This section will focus on the themes of justice and revenge in the Underworld and examine the structure of the Book.

Task: Comprehending Book Eleven

Read Book Eleven of the Odyssey

Once you have, write brief responses to the following questions;

- *Consider the structural differences between Book Eleven and other books of the Odyssey.*
- *What has Homer focussed on in Book Eleven?*

Characters in Book Eleven

The following characters are present in Book Eleven;

- *Odysseus*
- *Elpenor, an unfortunate Ithacan*
- *Eurylochus an Ithacan*
- *Perimedes, an Ithacan*
- *Teiresias, the blind seer*
- *Anticleia, Odysseus' mother*
- *Arete*
- *Alcinous*
- *Echeneus*
- *Agamemnon*
- *Achilles*
- *Ajax*
- *Heracles*

Book Eleven: Synopsis

In Book Eleven, Odysseus travels to the Underworld to seek the knowledge of the dead prophet Teiresias. Odysseus sails to the gateway of the Underworld and speaks to a parade of the illustrious dead. Teiresias tells Odysseus how to get home; he will face perils, but so long as he and his men do not eat the cattle of Hyperion all will be well.

The Structure of Book Eleven

Book Eleven of the *Odyssey* can most easily be divided into the following sections;

- *Elpenor and arrival at the Underworld (lines 1-85)*

- *Teiresias and Anticleia (lines 86-233)*

- *The parade of illustrious women (lines 234-331)*

- *Intermission (lines 332-385)*

- *The heroic Greeks (lines 386-566)*

- *The parade of illustrious men (lines 567-608)*

- *Heracles (609-end)*

Task: Descriptive language of the Underworld

Read Book Eleven

Identify descriptive passages in Book Eleven. Explore the language used by Homer to describe the scenes in the Underworld?

How do these descriptive passages enhance the experience for the audience?

The structure of Book Eleven

It has been debated whether Book Eleven was part of the original epic of the *Odyssey*. This debate has been caused in part due to some of the textual and linguistic peculiarities it contains, which will not be elaborated on further here, suffice to say that the core of this argument returns to whether or not there was an individual called Homer who did, or did not create the *Odyssey* and the *Iliad*.

Nevertheless, Book Eleven is an important part of the *Odyssey* and serves well the wider plot of Odysseus' journey and *Nostos* (Homecoming).

The structure is strictly controlled and broken down as follows;

The structure of Book Eleven

- **Part One -** The Journey into the Underworld and sacrifice of sheep for the Dead and encounters Elpenor. (Lines 1-85)
- **Part Two -** Odysseus speaks to Teiresias and his mother, Anticleia; he is informed of what to do in order to get home and what to do once he has arrived (Teiresias) and news of his family (Anticleia). (Lines 86-223)
- **Part Three -** Odysseus questions a range of noble women from the past and recalls their fate. (Lines 225-331)
- **Part Four -** 'The intermission'. The scene returns briefly to Phaeacia with interjections by Arete and Alcinous. (Lines 332-385)
- **Part Five -** 'The Heroic Greeks' – Odysseus speaks to Agamemnon, Achilles and tries to speak to Ajax. Agamemnon warns Odysseus to be cautious when he returns home and not to share his fate. Achilles asks Odysseus of news of his son and Ajax refuses to speak to Odysseus because Odysseus was judged to be the hero most worthy to bear the weapons and armour of Achilles. (Lines 386-566)
- **Part Six -** The catalogue of rewards and punishments of Hades. (Lines 566-609)
- **Part Seven -** Conversation with Heracles and Odysseus returns to the land of the living. (Lines 610-end)

Book Eleven is structured quite tightly. Bounded by the descent to and ascent from the Underworld, Odysseus meets two sets of important people. This is followed by the 'halfway point' or 'intermission' marked by a 'real-time' interjection from the audience of the story teller, Odysseus. This, we can imagine, would be in keeping to the poet as he recounts his tale with the interjection as a kind of encore. The tale resumes with Odysseus meeting his comrades from Troy and this leads in turn to Odysseus viewing the fate of other people after death as a result of their actions in life.

Elpenor and arrival at the Underworld (lines 1-85)

In the first part of Book Eleven Odysseus and his men set sail from the island of Aeaea with a favourable wind summoned by Circe. They sail to the edge of the world where the Cimmerians live in mist and fog.

Disembarking, Odysseus takes two men with him; Eurylochus and Perimedes as well as sacrificial victims. As soon as the sacrifice is complete, the dead swarm towards Odysseus, who keeps them at bay with his sword as he waits for the shade of the blind seer Teiresias.

As he waits though, the shade of Elpenor approaches. Odysseus is surprised to see him. He thought he was still on Aeaea. Elpenor tells the story of his death and pleads with Odyssues to ensure that he is buried and mourned correctly. This episode is an allusion to the episode in the Iliad when the ghost of Patroclus appeals to Achilles to bury his corpse.

Teiresias and Anticleia (lines 86-233)

Odysseus is now approached by the ghost of his mother Anticleia. Despite his yearning to speak to her, he nonetheless keeps his discipline and composure, and refuses to let her approach until he has spoken to Teiresias.

Teiresias now approaches and Odysseus allows him to drink the blood of the sacrificial victim. Once he has done this Teiresias informs Odysseus of the anger of Poseidon because of his blinding of Polyphemus. However, Teiresias gives Odysseus some glimmer of hope; if he and his men avoid killing the sacred cattle of the Sun God on the island of Thrinacie, then they will be able to return home.

If they do hurt the cattle, however, Odysseus' men will be doomed and he alone will return to Ithaca to face further trouble 'insolent men' in his own home. These men he will also overcome, but he will need to make amends to Poseidon by setting out on another adventure. He will need to head far inland to a find a people who have never heard of the sea. Once there he will need to plant an oar and sacrifice to Poseidon. After this his death will come in the distant future, in old age surrounded by a prosperous people.

Points to consider

What do you think is the significance of Odysseus' journey to the Underworld?

What can we learn about morality and the consequences of actions in Book Eleven?

Odysseus then speaks with his mother (again supplied with information of how to proceed by the prophet). Anticleia asks why Odysseus is here, in this place. Odysseus replies that he is here to try and find his way back to Ithaca. Odysseus also asks news of his mother news. How did his mother die? Is his father still alive? Is Penelope she still his wife or has she a new husband?

Anticleia responds to these questions in reverse order, the *'Homeric last-first'*. Penelope is still unmarried, Laertes is alive but living in poverty and Anticleia died of a broken heart; so much so did she miss her son. Anticleia's final words to her son are a simile; *'the soul slips away like a dream'* (line 220-221).

> **Remember!**
>
> Remember that Odysseus is telling a story through Books Nine and Twelve.

Task: The predictions of Teiresias

Reread the passage Book 11, lines 98-118:

From; *"I drew back, sheathing my silver-studded sword in its scabbard..*

To;

.. It is true that you will take revenge on these men for their misdeeds when you reach home." '

- ❖ To what extent do the predictions of Teiresias come true?
- ❖ Which of these predictions do we know already have come true?

The parade of illustrious women (lines 234-331)

What follows next is a digression. Odysseus observes and tells the stories of the illustrious women who he allows to drink of the sacrificial blood and tell him their stories. The women who he interviews are;

- Tyro, Antiope, Alcmene, Megare

- Epicaste (Jocasta), Chloris, Leda, Iphimedeia

- Phaedra, Procris, Ariadne

- Maera, Clymene, Eriphyle

Each has a short story associated with them that Homer has Odysseus relate to his audience.

Intermission (lines 332-385)

Homer now has Odysseus break his narrative and return to 'his' present; the Phaeacian palace. This is a unique occurrence in the *Odyssey*. Odysseus calls a pause in his story. Arete begins with a request to her lords to gift Odysseus well and this is seconded by Echeneus. Alcinous now speaks. He will reward Odysseus and send him home with gifts.

Odysseus is happy with this response. The granting of such gifts will ensure that he will gain respect and standing by returning with such gifts. Both the granting and receiving of gifts was for a Homeric hero an indication of his good *timé* and *kleos*.

Alcinous then speaks for the poet Homer himself; Odysseus is a fantastic storyteller and is urged to continue, which he does.

The heroic Greeks (lines 386-566)

Book Eleven provides Homer with the opportunity to revisit certain characters from the *Iliad*. Achilles, Agamemnon and Ajax all feature prominently in this book. Whilst two of these characters reveal to Odysseus tales of woe and despair, the third, Ajax, refuses to speak to Odysseus at all; a result of a grudge that continues even in death.

The *Iliad* is the product of one such grudge, the confrontation between Achilles and Agamemnon. In Book Eleven of the *Odyssey*, Odysseus departs from this theme and refuses to maintain the old hatreds of past events. He tries to speak to Ajax, with whom he quarrelled.

In the events that followed the *Iliad,* Odysseus and Ajax quarrel over who should have the armour of the dead Achilles. Odysseus wins the vote and Ajax tries to murder the Greek leaders that voted against him. He fails because he is thwarted by the deception of Athena and he instead slaughters a flock of sheep. This disgrace is too much for Ajax and he commits suicide. The Greek Tragedian Sophocles wrote a play called *Ajax* about this story.

The descent into the underworld also identifies Odysseus as being a hero. Who but a hero could visit the land of the dead and then return to the land of the living? This action is therefore in accord with Odysseus being a hero.

The face of Agamemnon? A burial mask from Mycenae, Greece

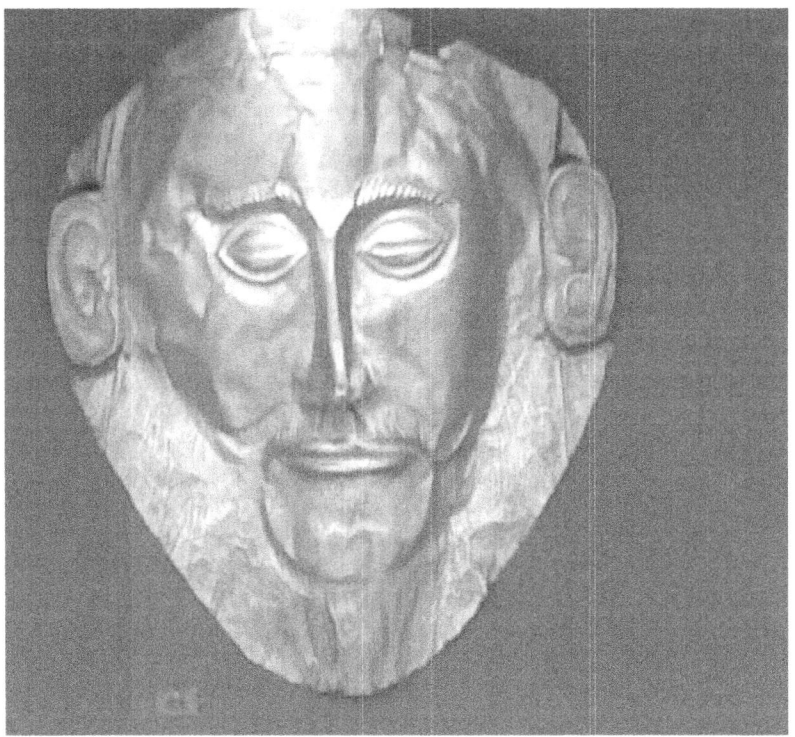

Agamemnon

Agamemnon now approaches. For Odysseus the sight of Agamemnon is a shock. He does not expect to see him here. Odysseus asks of Agamemnon's fate. What happened to him? Agamemnon tells Odysseus the story of his death. This story has already been related on several occasions in the Books of the Telemachy, but Agamemnon tells it more graphically. He and his men are slaughtered like livestock by Aegisthus at a feast. Agamemnon however most pities the death of Cassandra and his helplessness at being able to prevent her murder by his wife Clytemnestra.

Agamemnon warns Odysseus to beware of his wife Penelope; perhaps she is loyal, but perhaps she may not be. He advises

Odysseus to enter Ithaca secretly and explore the situation before he reveals his return. Agamemnon now requests news from Odysseus. What can he tell him of his son Orestes? Odysseus can unfortunately tell Agamemnon nothing regarding his son. However, Homer's audience already knows this information. Menelaus has told Telemachus that Orestes avenged his father.

Achilles and Ajax

> **Remember!**
>
> Hades was both the name of the King of the Underworld and the name of the Underworld also.

Achilles now approaches Odysseus. For Achilles, Odysseus is in the Underworld as a heroic exploit. What else is he planning? Odysseus tells Achilles the purpose of his visit and then praises Achilles as the most fortunate of men both alive and dead. Like Agamemon, Achilles asks for news of his son but here Odysseus can tell him a story from the Trojan War.

Homer then has Odysseus provide his audience with a digression on the bravery and wisdom of Neoptolemus as well as his battle prowess. This is good news for Achilles who retreats into the Underworld gladdened by the encounter.

Ajax however is another matter; he refuses to speak to Odysseus, carrying with him the anger and resentment he had against Odysseus in life into the afterlife.

As well as portraying Odysseus as a hero in a supernatural setting, the theme of justice can be seen at work in Book Eleven: Justice can clearly be seen at work amongst the inhabitants of Hades. Odysseus is admonished by Achilles for his self-pity (lines 480-491);

> ' "And do not make light of death, illustrious Odysseus", he replied.
>
> "I would rather work the soil as a serf on hire to some landless impoverished peasant than be King of all these lifeless dead.'
>
> *Book XI.488-491*

Although Odysseus may feel hard-done-by in his plight, he is still alive and the episode reminds him and his audience that justice *does* exist, because it is backed up by the gods, and he can see what happens to the dead. It is by their action that Odysseus' crew perish, and it is by his actions that Odysseus will see justice done when he arrives home.

In Hades, Odysseus is also permitted to witness the final consequences of one's actions in life, and what results from these actions. This should remind him that actions have consequences. Therefore Odysseus must choose wisely, whatever he does, or face the consequences.

The parade of illustrious men (lines 567-608)

Odysseus now briefly identifies a parade of illustrious men – some good men, some punished by the gods. This parade mirrors that of the illustrious women identified earlier in Book Eleven. Odysseus mentions;

- Minos, Orion
- Tityus, Tantalus, Sisyphus

This parade is much shorter and only the first two seem to have been honoured in the Underworld of Hades. The other three undergo severe and eternal punishments for their crimes against the Gods. These short digressions serve as a warning for Odysseus. He must make amends to Poseidon for injuring his son if he ever wants to escape from his problems.

Heracles (609-end)

The final section of Book Eleven is a visit by the wraith of Heracles to Odysseus. Heracles terrifies the spirits of the dead and his dress is likewise a collage of fighting, wild animals and massacre. Despite his fearsome appearance, Heracles greets Odysseus as a kindred spirit; working his way through a doom for a crime committed. Heracles however gives hope with his message; Heracles overcame his doom, so too will Odysseus, and it is by overcoming these challenges that Heracles became famous among men. With Heracles' departure, so too does Odysseus return to his ship.

Task: Odysseus and the Underworld

Write a response to the following question;

What do you think is the most important 'gain' for Odysseus during his visit to the Underworld?

Consider;

- The information he receives about his family
- The information on how to get home
- Confirmation of his heroic status

4.4 Book Twelve: The Cattle of the Sun

In this section we will;

- Explore the content and style of Book Twelve of the Odyssey

- Examine the theme of the supernatural in Book Twelve

- Examine the role of monsters in the Odyssey

- Examine the theme of justice and revenge in Book Twelve

- Explore the relationship between Odysseus and his men

- Consider the character of Eurylochus

- Consider some of the stylistic and structural techniques used by Homer

- Explore the ways in which Homer uses language to engage the audience

Book Twelve of the Odyssey

Book Twelve is the final section of the part of Odysseus' tale of his *Odyssey*. This topic focuses on the relationship between Odysseus and his men, the threat and peril of monsters and the divine punishment mete out by the Gods on the Ithacans when they kill and eat the sacred cattle of the Sun God.

> ### Task: Comprehending Book Twelve
>
> Read Book Twelve of the Odyssey
>
> Once you have, write brief responses to the following questions;
>
> - What has Homer focussed on in Book Twelve?
> - How does Odysseus and his crew interact with each other in this part of the Odyssey?

Characters in Book Twelve

The following characters are present in Book Eleven;

- *Odysseus*
- *Circe*
- *Sirens, a group of monsters*
- *Scylla, a monster*
- *Charybdis, a monstrous whirlpool*
- *Hyperion, the Sun God*
- *Zeus, an immortal*
- *Lampetie, daughter of Hyperion and a Nymph*

Book Twelve: Synopsis

In Book Twelve, Odysseus returns to Circe's island and bids her and Elpenor farewell. Setting sail, Odysseus avoids the perils of the Siren song and escapes the whirlpool of Charybdis by losing six men to the monster Scylla, but on reaching the island of the Sun God, they are marooned there by contrary winds. At last, the hungry Ithacans kill and eat some of Hyperion's cattle while they wait for the wind to change.

Setting sail at last, Hyperion threatens to take the sun to the Underworld if Zeus refuses to punish the Ithacans. Zeus strikes Odysseus' ship with a thunderbolt, destroying it and killing all of the Ithacans. Only Odysseus survives and he is washed up on the island of Ogygia where he spends the next seven years as a guest of Calypso.

The Structure of Book Twelve

Book Twelve of the *Odyssey* can most easily be divided into the following sections;

- *Return to Aeaea (lines 1-142)*

- *The Sirens (lines 143-200)*

- *Scylla and Charybdis (lines 201-260)*

- *The cattle of the Sun (lines 261-374)*

- *Divine punishment (lines 375-end)*

- *Odysseus and his men*

The structure of Book Twelve resembles the same structure of Books Nine and Ten. In Books Nine and Ten, there were two shorter dangers are followed by the main, longer episode and this pattern is continued in Book Twelve.

In Book Twelve, Odysseus first encounters the Sirens, loses some men in the dash past from Scylla and Charybdis, before finally the arrival on Thrinacie, an island sacred to the Sun God, Hyperion. The consumption of Hyperion's cattle condemns Odysseus' men to death. Only Odysseus survives, since he did not join his men in eating the sacred cattle.

In Book Nine, the Cyclops Polyphemus curses Odysseus and his men (IX, lines 527-535). Odysseus is unaware of this curse, although the audience of the *Odyssey* have been informed at the outset that his would occur. Indeed, the audience have been aware of this fate since the very beginning of the *Odyssey* where it is specifically mentioned in the *proem*;

> 'Tell me Muse, the story of that resourceful man who was driven to wander far
> and wide after he had sacked the holy citadel of Troy. He saw the cities of
> many people and he learnt there ways. He suffered great anguish on the high
> seas in his struggles to preserve his life and bring his comrades home. But he
> failed to save those comrades, in spite of all his efforts. It was their own
> transgression that bought them to their doom, for in their folly they devoured
> the oxen of Hyperion the Sun-god and he saw to it that they would never
> return. Odyssey

Book I.1-10

Return to Aeaea (lines 1-142)

Odysseus returns to Aeaea, and he and his men immediately locate and perform the burial rites for Elpenor; thus fulfilling the promise he made in Book Eleven.

Circe now is introduced in the scene. She now gives Odysseus detailed directions on how Odysseus can sail home. She describes the perils and gives advice on how to avoid tragedy when the ship reaches the Sirens, the Monster Scylla and the whirlpool Charybdis. Circe also warns Odysseus to avoid the island of Thrinacie, but if he *must* land, not to harm the animals there.

Given that Circe's information is this full and comprehensive, we may wonder why Odysseus bothered to go to the Underworld in Book Eleven. However, Circes does not tell Odysseus how to make amends to Poseidon; it is Teiresias who does this.

The Sirens (lines 143-200)

Odysseus sets sail with a favourable wind granted by Circe. Once on their way, Odysseus warns his crew in full what dangers they will face when they encounter the Sirens. Odysseus, however, desires to hear for himself what no-one else has and survived; the song of the Siren. He does this because he is a hero and the act will enhance his reputation.

Vase painting depicting the episode of Odysseus and the Sirens

Scylla and Charybdis (lines 201-260)

The next challenge to be faced is the twin perils of Scylla and Charybdis. The choice is easy, death for all, or death for six men. However Odysseus does not tell his crew this time of *all* of the perils that they face. He does not tell them that six men will die. On the one hand this is reasonable, after all what good would it do to tell them that some of them *will* die? However, Odysseus' men are all veterans of the Trojan War and survivors of the Cyclops, the Cicones and other perils. Maybe he should tell them exactly what peril they face.

The ship passes Scylla and six men are taken by the monster. Homer uses a simile to describe their fate; the men are like little fish caught by an angler (lines.250-260).

The cattle of the Sun (lines 261-374)

The ship now reaches Thrinacie; the island of the sun God. Odysseus warns his men not to land. However he finds himself overruled when Eurylochus convinces the rest of the crew. Odysseus then agrees to their decision but makes each man swear an oath that no-one hurts any animals they find.

The ship is kept at the island however. A storm prevents them from setting sail and after a month their food supplies are running low. Whilst Odysseus goes to pray alone, his men led by Eurylochus take matters into their own hands and they kill and eat some cattle. In return they promise to build Hyperion a temple on Ithaca. When Odysseus learns of this act, he is horrified as he now knows his men are doomed. Homer presents the meat of the sacred cattle spoiling, with a spectral lowing reaching their ears (lines 391-397).

Divine punishment (lines 375-end)

This act does not escape notice. The Nymph Lampetie informs Hyperion of this crime against him and Hyperion demands of Zeus justice. If he is refused he warns, Hyperion will take the Sun to the Underworld instead of its usual route across the sky.

Zeus agrees. Seven days after the storm ends, Odysseus and his men set sail, and soon are struck by a storm. Zeus then strikes the ship with lightning and all of Odysseus' men are killed. Only Odysseus survives astride the remains of his ship.

At first, he is taken back to Scylla and Charybdis, where Odysseus escapes from the whirlpool by allowing his 'raft' to be taken by the whirlpool whilst he sheltered on a rock with an olive tree. Here he waits until the timbers are spewed back out of the whirlpool. Odysseus then clings to the wreckage for nine days until he reaches the island of Ogygia and the Nymph Calypso.

Comparing the Suitors and the crew

Comparing the Suitors and the crew

Compare the actions of the Suitors in Books One through Four of the *Odyssey* with the description of the actions of Odysseus' men in this book Twelve, as well as the *proem*.

Do you notice any similarities or differences between the Suitors and the crew?

Despite never encountering each other, as well as being on one hand enemies of Odysseus, with the others being comrades, the Suitors and Odysseus' men share more similarities than differences.

Despite their wildly different circumstances and relationship to Odysseus, it is through their personal choices and the consequences of these choices that they are similar.

Both groups of men collectively abuse *xenia* throughout the *Odyssey*. Although individuals in both groups have some good qualities, both groups refuse to listen to sound advice that is offered them and both groups are guilty of disloyalty and insubordination towards Odysseus.

Throughout the *Odyssey* it is apparent that both groups will receive their rightful, god-ordained punishment due to the decisions and actions that they take. These groups are connected by a neat symmetry. The crew are drowned at the end of Book Twelve, halfway through the *Odyssey*.

The destruction of the crew anticipates that of the Suitors, which come towards the end of the *Odyssey*.

Eurylochus

Eurylochus is related to Odysseus and is his second in command. Despite this, he is characterised by almost consistent disobedience to Odysseus. He bears some resemblance to Odysseus in that he is crafty, and manages to avoid the trap set by Circe, which sees his group of men transformed into pigs. But if he is a reflection of Odysseus, he is a very vague one.

In Book Twelve, Eurylochus is more prominent; he has a persuasive tongue and convinces the crew to stop on the island of Hyperion; despite Odysseus' concern, he too is convinced. Eurylochus begins by complimenting Odysseus, making reference to his famed endurance *'whose spirit never flags and whose body never tires.'* (line 302). However, by comparing between the endurance of Odysseus and the lesser abilities of the rest of his men, Eurylochus is indeed suggesting that Odysseus is too hard on his crew. They need a break in order to recover their nerve and strength, and the island of Thrinacie is the ideal place, he thinks, to do this.

Eurylochus also appeals to Odysseus' practical nature, and suggests that stopping on the island is far better than to carry on sailing. There is some sense in what he says; it is foggy and the difficult conditions increase the risk of shipwreck, which is further increased by sailing at night, and through uncharted seas. The crew don't know where they can stop. Are there any friendly ports for them to stop at? Or will the next stop be like the disastrous stop in the lands of the Laestrygonians? (lines 301-318). In any event, he argues, they need only stay the night.

Eurylochus' suggestions *are* eminently sensible, and Odysseus agrees, providing they promise not to harm any animals they find on the island. However, the crew disobey Odysseus. Unable to leave because of contrary winds, they stay longer than the single night promised and, running short of food, end up slaughtering and eating the herds of the Sun-god. It is this crime against the God that results in their deaths.

Hyperion, Zeus and the death of Odysseus' crew.

The Sun-god Hyperion, also known as Helios, is the god that demands the deaths of Odysseus' crew. It is somewhat surprising that Homer has Hyperion, and not Poseidon, demanding the destruction of Odysseus' crew and ship.

Yet Hyperion does not act directly against Odysseus and his men. The punishment falls to *Zeus* (again, not Poseidon), who sends the storm that kills the crew (Book Twelve. lines 385-8). In this final act of the crew of Odysseus, Poseidon is absent among the Gods. Zeus, as Father of the Olympians, is responsible for upholding morality and correct behaviour. Since the men have offended Hyperion by eating his sacred cattle, they are punished by Zeus. Once again, and unwittingly or not, the crew of Odysseus have abused the *xenia* of the lord of the island of Thrinacie. They were allowed to take refuge on the island, but to harm the herds was a crime that could not go unpunished.

Hyperion demands that Zeus acts; if he does not, then Hyperion threatens to take the Sun to the Underworld and bring day there instead. Zeus promises to punish Odysseus and his crew and holds to his promise.

It is Zeus' ultimate responsibility to take charge over the affairs of mortals through the guardianship of the social 'glue' of the code of *xenia*. By harming the property of Hyperion, Odysseus' men bring down the punishment of Zeus, in much the same way, by abusing the property of the absent Odysseus, Zeus determines also that the Suitors shall pay the ultimate punishment for their actions.

Morality, Justice and Revenge in the *Odyssey*

Do Odysseus' crew truly deserve the punishment for the crime which they committed on the isle of the Sun-god? After all, the men only eat the herds of Hyperion once their own food is exhausted. They face starvation and determine to make amends once they return home by the construction of a huge temple to Hyperion, if they survive the wrath they know they will bring on themselves.

Unfortunately for the crew, they cannot use ignorance as a defence. Odysseus' men were warned, and on more than one occasion.

In Book XI, lines 110-120, Book XII, lines 137-154 and again in Book XII, lines 320-330 warnings are made about eating the cattle. Odysseus makes the crew swear an oath at Book XII, line 303 and the crew demonstrate that they commit their deed in full knowledge that it is wrong at Book XII, lines 365-378.

To compound this crime, the crew do not even carry out the ritual of sacrifice to the gods properly, short of the proper vestments, the crew use water and fresh green leaves rather than wine and barley as is proper. Since the slaughter of the cattle is offensive to Hyperion, so too is the manner in which the crew make sacrificial rites to the gods.

Both the crew and the Suitors have their own fate in their hands, and it is their actions that determine their fate. Harsh though these may seem; they are also necessary. Without the actions of both crew and Suitors, Homer would not have a story of Odysseus' *'Nostos'* (homecoming) and the audience would be denied the *Odyssey*.

Task: Exam style response

Write a 3-4 paragraph response to the following question;

To what extent do Odysseus **and** his men deserve the criticism that they acted with 'senseless stupidity' on their travels?

You might include discussion of:

- The loss of the men at the hands of the Cicones and Laestrygonians
- Delay with the Lotus Eaters
- The adventures with Polyphemus, Aeolus and Circe
- The passing of the Sirens, Scylla and Charybdis
- The final death of all the crew

Part Five: Odysseus in Ithaca

Part Five: Odysseus in Ithaca

5.1 Book Thirteen: Odysseus and the Gods

5.2 Book Fourteen: Eumaeus

5.3 Book Fifteen: Telemachus returns

5.4 Book Sixteen: Odysseus and Telemachus

Odysseus in Ithaca

Odysseus sets off from the island of the Phaeacians in one of their ships, with vast amounts of treasure bestowed upon him by his hosts. Odysseus lands in Ithaca and his treasure is hidden in a cave.

Odysseus meets Athena who advises that he avoid the palace for the moment, but instead goes to visit Eumaeus, a loyal swineherd and learn more of what he faces.

Eumaeus welcomes Odysseus, who arrives disguised as a Cretan hero who has suffered much misfortune and offers him the hospitality of a common man. Here he learns of the Suitors and their actions.

Telemachus returns to Ithaca and is brought by Athena to Eumaeus' farm. Odysseus at first continues his disguise to his son, but is then revealed to his son and the pair are tearfully reunited.

5.1 Book Thirteen: Odysseus and the Gods

In this section we will;

- *Explore the content and style of Book Thirteen of the Odyssey*

- *Understand the role of the Immortals in the Odyssey*

- *Explore the theme of justice and revenge in the Odyssey*

- *Continue to explore the importance of xenia*

- *Consider the relationship between Odysseus and Athena in the Odyssey*

- *Consider some of the stylistic and structural techniques used by Homer*

- *Explore the ways in which Homer uses language to engage the audience*

Book Thirteen of the *Odyssey*

In Book Thirteen, Odysseus now takes his leave of the Phaeacians and arrives back in Ithaca.

Task: Comprehending Book Thirteen

Read Book Thirteen of the Odyssey

Once you have, write brief responses to the following questions;

- *How is Odysseus presented in Book Thirteen?*
- *What is Odysseus' attitude towards Athena in this Book?*

> ### *Characters in Book Thirteen*
>
> *The following characters are present in Book Thirteen;*
>
> - *Odysseus*
> - *Alcinous, Lord of the Phaeacians*
> - *Poseidon, God of the Sea*
> - *Zeus, King of the Gods*
> - *Athena, the patron Goddess of Odysseus*

Book Thirteen: Synopsis

In Book Thirteen, Odysseus leaves the island of the Phaeacians in one of their ships, with vast amounts of treasure bestowed upon him by his hosts. Odysseus lands in Ithaca and his treasure is hidden in a cave.

Odysseus meets Athena and realising who she is, converses with her. Athena advises that he avoid the palace for the moment, but instead goes to visit Eumaeus, a loyal swineherd and learn more of what he faces.

The Structure of Book Thirteen

Book Thirteen of the *Odyssey* can most easily be divided into the following sections;

- Farwell to the Phaeacians (lines 1-124)

- Poseidon and Zeus (lines 125-187)

- Odysseus and Athena (lines 187-end)

Task: Comprehending and analysing Book Thirteen

If you haven't already done so read Book Thirteen, and as you do so, write responses to the following questions;

Read Book 13, Lines 1-69

1. What rituals typical of *xenia* are shown here? Pick out two examples.

Read Book 13, Lines 70-124

2. Odysseus travels from the fantasy land of the Phaeacians to the real place of Ithaca in these lines. Describe four details of his journey.

Read Book 13, Lines 125-187

3. Poseidon punishes the Phaeacians for helping Odysseus return home.

Consider what Poseidon is most upset by.

Read Book 13, Lines 188-228

4. Odysseus awakens on Ithaca. What language does Homer use to illustrate Odysseus' first impressions?

Read Book 13, Lines 228-427

5. How does Odysseus first introduce himself to Athena?

6. What characteristics of Odysseus do we see from his dealings with Athena?

7. What kind of relationship do Athena and Odysseus have?

Read Book 13, Lines 429-end:

8. How is Odysseus disguised by Athena?

Farwell to the Phaeacians (lines 1-124)

Odysseus has now finished the story of his trials and tribulations since leaving Troy and being kept as a virtual prisoner by Calypso. Alcinous orders a banquet prepared and personally stores treasures and supplies on the ship that will transport Odysseus before personally sacrificing an ox in honour of Zeus. Alcinous also issues instructions for the Phaeacians to gift Odysseus treasures; bronze tripods and cauldrons – valuable gifts. Odysseus is impatient to be off and Homer deploys a nice simile to illustrate this in lines 30-33; Odysseus is like a ploughman that yearns for his supper.

Odysseus then makes a speech which is polite but clear; he wants to leave, but he prays that those he leaves behind will experience great happiness (lines 38-69). This speech is very well received by the Phaeacians and Alcinous performs the rites of farewell that are associated with perfect *xenia.*

Odysseus boards the ship and sleeps as the Phaeacians sail him home to Ithaca and Homer again deploys a series of linguistic techniques to describe and illustrate the movement of the ship and the man which it bears back to Ithaca (lines 81-92).

Homer then describes the landing on the island of Ithaca. The Phaeacians deposit Odysseus and his treasure at a secluded harbour and a cave sacred to the Nymphs. (lines 93-123) It is here that the Phaeacians carefully offload the slumbering Odysseus and his treasure.

Poseidon and Zeus (lines 125-187)

What follows now is a scene shift by Homer. The poet describes how Poseidon witnesses the arrival of Odysseus in Ithaca, and how it is that his own descendants, the Phaeacians, have transported him home. Poseidon is insulted and offended. He clearly states (lines 130-132) that he never intended to prevent Odysseus from reaching Ithaca; he never intended to kill the hero for example, but Poseidon clearly did not want Odysseus to reach home just yet and certainly not escorted by Poseidon's own descendants and with a huge hall of treasure. Poseidon complains to Zeus and is given permission to punish the Phaeacians for their actions.

Poseidon's decision is to turn the ship to stone in sight of the island of Scherie and also to ring the island in mountains so that the

Phaeacians can never leave again. Zeus mitigates this act and recommends that only the ship should be turned into a mountain; fulfilling the prophecy mentioned by Alcinous, but otherwise leaving the Phaeacians unharmed. This is done and witnessed by the Phaeacians, who correctly interpret the anger of Poseidon and duly offer him a large sacrifice in compensation.

Odysseus and Athena (lines 187-end)

After this digression among the Immortals, Homer now returns the focus of the story to Ithaca. Odysseus awakens and his first thoughts are that he has been fooled after all by the Phaeacians. He does not recognise where he is because Athena has obscured the island in a mist. Odysseus' speech in lines 200-216 has some similarities to the one he made when he arrived on Scherie in Book Six. This time however he is more concerned about his treasure. He needs to hide it.

Athena now appears to Odysseus disguised as a shepherd. Odysseus asks where he is. Athena reveals that he has indeed landed on Ithaca, much to Odysseus' joy.

Despite suspecting who he addresses, Odysseus spins Athena a tall tale about who he is and where he comes from (Lines 250-290). He says he is a Cretan exile who had killed Idomeneus' son Orsilochus, and had now been left marooned by the crew of a Phoenician ship. This story will be retold with embellishments and alterations through much of the remainder of the *Odyssey*. It appears that even at the outset, Odysseus is planning to be cunning and deceptive whilst he explores the situation on Ithaca.

Calling his bluff, Athena warns Odysseus of the dangers of confronting the Suitors. Odysseus and Athena instead plan how to overcome the Suitors. This episode demonstrates the extent of Odysseus' independence and guile; he will even lie to the goddess in order to ensure that she will assist him. This is one of the strengths of the *Odyssey*; Odysseus is a character who is allowed to demonstrate his skills and abilities. Odysseus is not some puppet of the gods, useless and helpless without their intervention.

One incident in Book Thirteen deserves further mention; once Athena has revealed herself to Odysseus, the hero of the *Odyssey* wastes little time in asking Athena quite sharply why she hasn't helped him earlier;

> *"I did not notice you then, Daughter of Zeus, nor see you set foot*
> *on my ship to save me from some of my ordeals".*
>
> *Book XIII.318-320.*

Odysseus is both respectful yet forceful with his patron deity. He wants to know why Athena hadn't helped him and why she hadn't helped to spare his crew. In this response, Odysseus is voicing the unanswered prayers of many in the ancient world, who had prayed and sacrificed and yet the gods had seemed not to listen.

Athena replies somewhat weakly that she knew Odysseus would get home eventually and also acknowledges that she was unwilling or unable to confront Poseidon over his anger against Odysseus.

The role of Athena in the *Odyssey*

The goddess Athena (or Athene) was the patron deity of crafts and of war in the ancient Greek pantheon. Throughout both the *Iliad* and the *Odyssey*, Athena is the god that favours Odysseus above all others. In the *Iliad* Athena was keen to take an active role in protecting her chosen favourites, often the goddess would stand side by side with them in battle.

Despite this warlike nature, which obviously would appeal to the ancient Greek men who aspired to emulate their heroes, Athena also shared characteristics with women. Athena was as famed for her craft skills such as weaving. Athena was also a virgin goddess and seen as the protector of cities. In particular Athena was held as the guardian goddess of Athens.

Athens was unique amongst the Greek city states in that she was named after an Olympian deity, and it is no surprise then that the Athenians held Athena in particular veneration.

Athena is perhaps the most important immortal in the *Odyssey*. It is Athena that sends Telemachus on his journey in the *Telemachy*; it is Athena that convinces Zeus to order the release of Odysseus from the island of Calypso. It is fair to say that without the intercession of Athena, Odysseus will not achieve his goal of returning home, his *'Nostos'*. Finally, it is Athena that brings Odysseus to the palace of Alcinous on the island of the Phaeacians.

Another thing to note is the absence of Athena from Books Nine to Twelve. Odysseus undergoes all of his trials and tribulations of these books without the assistance of Athena, this absence is notable, for as Odysseus cannot fail when he has the goddess by his side, when she is absent, Odysseus suffers.

Poseidon

Poseidon was the Greek god of the sea, earthquakes and also of horses; the god of the sea was widely worshipped in the Ancient Greek world. In art, Poseidon was typically portrayed as a sombre, mature male and without his trident, is often mistaken for Zeus.

Take Note!

References to Poseidon's anger towards Odysseus in the *Odyssey* include;

Book I.20-21

Book I.68-75

Book V.284-290

Book XI.100-103

Book XIII.130-138

As brother to Zeus, Poseidon was considered to be one of the strongest Olympians, and like all brothers, the pair often had their arguments and disputes. Whilst acknowledging that Zeus is the lord of the Olympians, Homer typically presents Poseidon as a god that will be disobedient to Zeus' will if it suits him.

In the Iliad, Poseidon ignores Zeus' command to assist the Greeks whilst Zeus has granted temporary favour to the Trojans. Likewise in the *Odyssey*, Poseidon's anger with Odysseus is also at odds with Zeus' will that Odysseus will eventually get back to Ithaca. This also puts him at odds with Athena. In several Greek myths Athena and Poseidon squabble, perhaps the most famous of these disputes being the contest for the patronage of Athens.

Poseidon and the punishment of Odysseus

As has already been stated, Poseidon is angered by Odysseus because of the injury he had inflicted on Polyphemus the Cyclops, who is the son of the god of the sea. Before this event occurs Poseidon bears Odysseus no particular ill will. In Book XIII, lines 130-132 Poseidon explains his actions to Zeus;

> *" I said that Odysseus would suffer much before he reached his*
> *home, though I never put a final ban on his return, once you had*
> *promised it and nodded your assent."*

Despite being determined to punish Odysseus, Poseidon never tries to *kill* Odysseus, yet this is surely in his power to do so if he chose. After all, the audience of Homer would have been aware that in another Greek myth, a hero who had fought at Troy, 'little Ajax', was killed for his insolence and crimes against Poseidon when he had almost returned to his home after the war. In the *Odyssey*, Poseidon is eager to punish Odysseus for his wounding of Polyphemus, but once Odysseus reaches Ithaca, Poseidon's role in the *Odyssey* ends.

Poseidon's punishment is reserved for the Phaeacians; he transforms the ship and its crew into a mountain in the harbour of Scherie (the home of the Phaeacians). This leads to Alcinous recalling a prophecy that this would occur, appeasement is made by the Phaeacians, swearing to Poseidon that never again will they help a stranger home.

Making amends to Poseidon

In Book Eleven of the *Odyssey* we have already discussed how Odysseus receives instructions on how to make amends to the god who he had angered. Once Odysseus has dealt with the Suitors, the dead prophet Teiresias tells Odysseus that he cannot yet rest;

Take Note!
This tale that no doubt could have developed from this instruction is not part of the *Odyssey*, nevertheless, the episode serves to identify the *Odyssey* within a wider cycle of epics concerning the adventures of Odysseus.

> *"...you must set out once more. Take a well-cut oar and go on till*
> *you reach a people who know nothing of the sea and never use salt*
> *with their food...When you fall in with some other traveller who*
> *refers to the object you are carrying on your shoulder as a*
> *'winnowing fan', then plant your shapely oar in the earth and offer*
> *Lord Poseidon the sacrifice of a ram, a bull and a breeding boar.".*
>
> *Book XI.121-131*

5.2 Book Fourteen: Eumaeus

In this section we will;

- *Explore the content and style of Book Fourteen of the Odyssey*

- *Begin to understand the role of Eumaus the Odyssey*

- *Explore the theme of storytelling in the Odyssey*

- *Explore the importance of disguise in this part of the Odyssey*

Book Fourteen of the *Odyssey*

In Book Fourteen, Odysseus arrives at a farm run by Eumaus; a swineherd and loyal servant of the family of Odysseus.

Task: Comprehending Book Fourteen

Read Book Fourteen of the Odyssey

Once you have, write brief responses to the following questions;

- *How is Odysseus presented in Book Fourteen?*
- *How is Eumaeus presented in Book Fourteen?*

Characters in Book Fourteen

The following characters are present in Book Fourteen;

- *Odysseus*
- *Eumaeus; a swineherd*

Book Fourteen: Synopsis

In Book Fourteen Odysseus reaches the farmstead of Eumaeus. Eumaeus is a swineherd, he raises pigs for the estate of Odysseus. As a result he is now one of the farmers that supplies the Suitors every day and therefore knows a great deal of what is going on in the palace.

Eumaeus therefore if a great source of information for Odysseus, so long as he is still loyal to Odysseus' family. Athena has told Odysseus that Eumaeus is loyal, but he decides to confirm this himself. Odysseus does not reveal his true identity to Eumaeus and much of Book Fourteen is taken up with Odysseus' storytelling.

The Structure of Book Fourteen

Book Fourteen of the *Odyssey* can most easily be divided into the following sections;

- *Odysseus arrives at the farm (lines 1-98)*

- *Exploring Eumaeus' character (lines 99-190)*

- *Odysseus' story (lines 191-359)*

- *Odysseus tests Eumaeus (360-end)*

Odysseus arrives at the farm (lines 1-98)

Homer begins Book Fourteen with a description of Eumaeus' farm and his livestock. There are many pigs here; some three hundred and sixty of them, guarded by four dogs, savage as wild beasts. Odysseus spots the swineherd making a pair of shoes, his four attendants are absent on choirs.

> **Task: Homer speaks to Eumaeus**
>
> Alone among all the characters present in the Odyssey, Homer speaks directly to Eumaeus. Why do you think he might do this?

Odysseus approaches the farm disguised as an old beggar and is confronted by the dogs. Rather than panicking Odysseus reacts calmly and waits for the swineherd to investigate. The first impression we have of Eumaeus' farm is a working farm in good order, its owner competent at what he does.

Eumaeus' first words reveal much about himself to Odysseus and Homer's audience. Despite Odysseus being disguised as a seedy old beggar, Eumaeus offers him hospitality and also reveals that he is loyal to Odysseus, *'the best of masters'* and he resents feeding his hogs to the suitors on a daily basis.

In line 55, Homer changes his style in relation to Eumaeus. Homer speaks to him directly; something he does not do with any other character in the *Odyssey*. Eumaeus reiterates his welcoming nature and gives an excellent overview of the good practice of xenia and also how a good lord (like Odysseus) should look after his loyal servants. He holds Helen responsible for his master's loss, who he now fears is dead, because of his participation in the Trojan War. Over a meal of freshly slaughtered piglet, Eumaeus also reveals his thoughts on the suitors. It is clear that he strongly disapproves of their actions.

Exploring Eumaeus' character (lines 99-190)

In lines 99-190 Eumaeus and Odysseus converse about the situation on Ithaca and about Eumaeus' master.

Task: Comprehending the character of Eumaeus in Book Fourteen

If you haven't already done so read Book Fourteen, lines 99-190, and as you do so, write responses to the following questions;

What is Eumaeus view of Odysseus?

What is his view of liars?

What does Odysseus swear in these lines?

What is Eumaeus' response?

What does Odysseus learn from Eumaeus in these lines?

Odysseus' story (lines 199-359)

Odysseus now tells Eumaeus a story. This story is a lie, a construct invented by Odysseus and an extended development of the story he told to Athena in Book Thirteen. But it also contains elements of truth. Odysseus claims he his born in Crete, the son of a rich man and a concubine. Odysseus claims to be a good warrior, that he was a naval captain and that he also commanded armies. As a result of these talents, he became wealthy.

Odysseus tells Eumaeus that he participated in the Trojan War and subsequently returned to Crete. He then decided to sail to Egypt and reached the river Nile. Here his men raid against orders and are killed. He alone is saved by the Egyptian king with whom he stays for eight years.

A Phoenician then takes him home for a year before taking his guest to Libya. Ship-wrecked 'Odysseus' survives, and finds himself in the land of Thresprotia, a historically identified location in NW Greece. Here he hears news of Odysseus – he has been to the oracle at Dodona (a historical site and religious sanctuary almost as prominent as Olympia to the Ancient Greeks). At Dodona, Odysseus sought instruction on how to return to Ithaca. Meantime 'Odysseus' escaped from slavers and arrived on Ithaca.

Like any good lie, this story does contain several truths;

- 'Odysseus' is a good fighter, sailor and leader of armies

- 'Odysseus' did take part in the Trojan War

- 'Odysseus' lost his men in a series of battles and misfortunes

- 'Odysseus' was a guest of someone for many years

Odysseus tests Eumaeus (360-end)

Eumaeus believes the tale of his guest but is sceptical of this story about his master in Thresprotia. He must have been lost at sea. Eumaeus now cleverly tells a story of a man who lied to him about Odysseus returning. He continues to offer his hospitality, but he does warn his guest not to lie.

Odysseus then makes a wager with Eumaeus. If his story is true, Eumaeus will give Odysseus clothes and send him on his way. If however Odysseus is proven to be lying – that Odysseus will not return, then Eumaeus can kill him. Eumaeus is horrified and refuses the wager and instead offers more food, giving his guest the portion of honour to *'a man like me'*.

Odysseus now tests Eumaeus with another story. He tells a war story from Troy. Whilst on a raid he forgot to take his cloak and being afraid he might freeze. He seeks the advice of Odysseus, who fools a man into heading back to camp with a message, this messenger leaves his cloak behind in order to run quickly and his cloak is taken by 'Odysseus'.

As they prepare to sleep, Eumaeus covers his guest with a thick cloak, to warm him through the night.

Task: The gift of a cloak

What do you think is the significance of the episode of the cloak?

5.3 Book Fifteen: Telemachus returns

In this section we will;

- *Explore the content and style of Book Fifteen of the Odyssey*

- *Continue to understand the theme of xenia the Odyssey*

- *Explore the theme of storytelling in the Odyssey*

- *Consider the treatment of women in the Odyssey*

- *Consider the theme of the role of Athena in Book Fifteen*

Book Fifteen of the *Odyssey*

In Book Fifteen, Homer adopts a two scene approach. In the first part of Book Fifteen, Homer returns to the story of Telemachus, who is still in Sparta but Telemachus returns home. In the second part of Book Fifteen, Homer switches back to Odysseus. In this topic we will explore the theme of xenia and also the importance of storytelling.

Task: Comprehending Book Fifteen

Read Book Fifteen of the Odyssey

Once you have, write brief responses to the following questions;

- *How is Telemachus presented in Book Fifteen?*
- *How important is the theme of xenia?*
- *How is Eumaeus presented in Book Fifteen?*

Characters in Book Fifteen

The following characters are present in Book Fifteen;

- *Telemachus*
- *Athena*
- *Peisistratus*
- *Menelaus*
- *Helen*
- *Megapenthes, son of Menelaus*
- *Eteoneus, squire of Menelaus*
- *Theoclymenus, an exiled seer*
- *Odysseus*
- *Eumaeus; a swineherd*
- *Peiraeus, a comrade of Telemachus*

Book Fifteen: Synopsis

In Book Fifteen, Homer adopts a two scene approach. In the first part of Book Fifteen, Homer returns to the story of Telemachus, who is still in Sparta but Telemachus returns home. In the second part of Book Fifteen, Homer switches back to Odysseus. Still in disguise he decides that he will go into the city. Homer also tells his audience more about the origins of Eumaeus before recounting the arrival of Telemachus in Ithaca.

The Structure of Book Fifteen

Book Fifteen of the Odyssey can most easily be divided into the following sections;

- *Telemachus (lines 1-220)*

- *Theoclymenus (lines 221-299)*

- *Odysseus and Eumaeus (lines 300-495)*

- *Telemachus returns to Ithaca (lines 496-end)*

Telemachus (lines 1-299)

Homer begins Book Fifteen by shifting the scene back to Telemachus, who was last seen back in Book Four. Telemachus is still in Sparta having trouble sleeping in the palace of Menelaus. Athena visits Telemachus openly and commands him to return home. She makes this command an urgent one, if Telemachus does not hurry home he may find not only is his mother married to Eurymachus, but she may carry off all the wealth of the palace also.

Athena also warns Telemachus that the Suitors are planning to ambush him at sea. However, Telemachus is assured that he will avoid them. He is further instructed not to return to the palace, but instead to head to the farm of Eumaeus.

Telemachus is all for setting off straightaway. However Peisistratus persuades him to allow Menelaus to send him off properly with gifts and a meal.

Menelaus duly agrees to let Telemachus leave, but ensures that he has fabulous gifts and a meal. This is another instance of the correct use of xenia. Menelaus gifts Telemachus a drinking cup, a mixing bowl and a robe for Helen to give to his wife when he marries. Homer spends some time illustrating the scene of this farewell.

The portrayal of Penelope in Book Fifteen

How is Penelope portrayed by Athena at the beginning of Book Fifteen?

How consistent is this portrayal from what we have seen in other parts of the Odyssey?

Telemachus and Peisistratus then set off, riding rapidly to Pylos in a chariot. When they arrive at Pylos however, Telemachus requests that Peisistratus let him set sail immediately. If Nestor discovered that Telemachus had returned he would undoubtedly delay him.

Peistratus agrees reluctantly, but he knows Nestor will be offended. This episode reveals Telemachus sense of urgency in getting home. It also enables Homer to avoid repeating the scenes he had already described in some detail earlier in this section of the *Odyssey*. For Homer, it is more important to get Telemachus back to what is now the focus of the action; Ithaca.

Theoclymenus (lines 221-299)

As Telemachus' ship is about to set sail, he is approached by a stranger. This is Theoclymenus, a seer the son of Melampus, who has already been mentioned in Book XI (line. 291). Theoclymenus seeks sanctuary. He is guilty of killing a relative and wants to escape punishment. Despite his guilt, Telemachus does not hesitate to accept and offers Theoclymenus the hospitality of Ithaca.

Theoclymenus will have a role to play later in the *Odyssey*, but this episode enables Telemachus to demonstrate his own good practice of xenia. He has learned much from his visit to Menelaus and Nestor and now is demonstrating that he is becoming a man and a leader.

Odysseus and Eumaeus (lines 300-495)

Homer now shifts the scene back to the farm of Eumaeus, where Odysseus is still present. Odysseus announces that he plans to go to the city and the palace. Perhaps he can beg or even find employment (remember he is still disguised as a beggar). Eumaeus advises against this – Odysseus will suffer abuse or worse, especially at the hands of the Suitors and their servants. Instead, Eumaeus urges that Odysseus remain with him. Once Telemachus returns it would be safer to go to the palace.

Odysseus now seeks information about Laertes and Anticleia; his parents. In some ways this information is redundant. Odysseus has already spoken to his mother in the Underworld, and knows something of the position of his father. Eumaeus praises Odysseus' parents and through him Homer elaborates somewhat on their background.

Odysseus now asks of Eumaeus *his* story and Eumaeus is happy to oblige. In lines 389-495 Homer has Eumaeus recount a lengthy story of *his* origins and how he arrived in Ithaca. As he makes clear he was not *always* a servant.

Eumeaus' father was Ctesius was king of the island of Syrie (a mythical place). One of the palace slaves, a Phoenician, is seduced by a crewman from a ship from Phoenicia. Together they stole wealth from Ctesius' house and also his son, Eumaeus, in order to pay for her escape. The woman was killed for this crime by the

Goddess Artemis, who shot her down with a sudden arrow. The Phoenicians then sold Eumaeus to Laertes when they landed in Ithaca.

Task: The character of Eumaeus in Book Fifteen

If you haven't already done so read Book Fifteen, lines 389-495, and as you do so, write responses to the following questions;

What is Eumaeus background?

In what ways does his story differ or is similar to the story given by Odysseus in Book Fourteen?

How are Phoenicians portrayed in this story?

How are women portrayed in this story?

Telemachus returns to Ithaca (lines 496-end)

Telemachus arrives back in Ithaca. However, he obeys the advice of Athena and decides to visit Eumaeus. He takes care not to neglect his guest however. Eumaeus' house is no place to entertain his guest, and besides, it is not his house to insist on this either. So Telemachus asks his comrade Peiraeus to look after Theoclymenus whilst he is away.

Eumaeus

Homer chooses to draw Eumaeus fairly fully. Despite being a slave, Eumaeus comes from a royal family. Sold by Phoenician slavers to Odysseus' father, he once lived in the palace as a companion for Odysseus' sister, but has since been established in a country house where he has prospered and even owns a slave himself. This distinguishes Eumaeus from the slaves of the house and other servants. In this respect, Eumaeus is not typical, since he is afforded a personality of his own rather than the status of human tool.

Eumaeus is a good and loyal slave to his lord and his family. Like Eurycleia, the elderly maid, Eumaeus' loyalty stands in stark contrast to many of Odysseus' other slaves. He is loyal, faithful and dutiful, but has found little favour with the new masters of Ithaca, the

Suitors and so had no dealing with them, unlike another slave, Melanthius, who is encountered later.

Eumaeus' character demonstrates warmth of character, as well as generosity of spirit. He elects to show hospitality to the disguised Odysseus, when he could have so easily showed meanness and driven Odysseus from his home.

Task: Eumeaus in Book Fifteen

Write a response to the following questions;

To what extent do you agree with the view that Book Fifteen is the Book of Eumaeus?

5.4 Book Sixteen: Odysseus and Telemachus

In this section we will;

- *Explore the content and style of Book Sixteen of the Odyssey*

- *Explore the theme of storytelling in the Odyssey*

- *Consider the relationship of son and father in the Odyssey*

- *Consider the role of Athena in Book Sixteen*

Book Sixteen of the Odyssey

In Book Sixteen, Odysseus is finally reunited with his son Telemachus. The scene for this reunion is the farm of Eumaeus and some for the language used by Homer is powerful. Homer then shifts the scene back to the palace where the Suitors and Penelope all hear the news that Telemachus has returned.

Task: Comprehending Book Sixteen

Read Book Sixteen of the Odyssey

Once you have, write brief responses to the following questions;

- *How is Telemachus presented in Book Sixteen?*
- *How does Odysseus reveal his identity to Telemachus?*
- *What linguistic techniques does Homer use in this book?*

Characters in Book Sixteen

The following characters are present in Book Sixteen;

- *Odysseus*
- *Telemachus*
- *Eumaeus*
- *Athena*
- *Penelope*
- *Eurymachus, a suitor*
- *Antinous, a suitor*
- *Amphinous, a suitor*

Book Sixteen: Synopsis

Like in Book Fifteen, in Book Sixteen Homer adopts a two scene approach. In the first part of Book Fifteen, Homer reunites Odysseus. Homer then switches the scene to the palace. It is here that the suitors and Penelope receive the news that Telemachus has returned before switching the scene back to the farm where Odysseus, Telemachus and Eumaeus eat.

The Structure of Book Sixteen

Book Sixteen of the Odyssey can most easily be divided into the following sections;

- *Telemachus arrives (lines 1-154)*

- *Odysseus and Telemachus are reunited (lines 155-320)*

- *In the Palace (lines 321-450)*

- *Eumaeus returns (lines 451-end)*

Telemachus arrives (lines 1-154)

Homer begins Book Sixteen with Odysseus and Eumaeus. They are having breakfast when Telemachus arrives. He is a familiar sight at Eumaeus' farm and the dogs welcome him. Eumaeus greets Telemachus warmly and Homer uses a simile to illustrate their close relationship. Eumaeus is 'like a father' to the returning Telemachus. Odysseus greets Telemachus politely, but without words, and gives no indication that he is Telemachus' long lost father. Telemachus asks Eumaeus who this stranger is and being told of some of his origins by Eumaeus offers to feed and clothe the stranger – but is reluctant to bring him to the palace as he feels he has little authority there.

Odysseus first speaks in line 90 – he asks Telemachus why he has no support. Have the people rejected him? Odysseus then ventures his opinion. *If he were* Odysseus, he would fight.

Telemachus replies that the people have no grievance, but he has little support. Telemachus does however ask Eumaeus to go to the palace and let his mother know that he has returned safely. Penelope then could also send this news to Laertes, who should also know of Telemachus' return.

Odysseus and Telemachus are reunited (lines 155-320)

As Eumaeus leaves on his mission, Athena arrives, invisible to Telemachus, but visible to the dogs and also to Odysseus. Odysseus goes outside to speak to the Goddess. Athena commands Odysseus to reveal his true identity to Telemachus so that they can plot the destruction of the suitors together. Athena then removes Odysseus disguise and restores his youthful physique.

When Odysseus re-enters the farmhouse, Telemachus thinks at first that he has been joined by a God (lines 181-185). Odysseus quickly refutes this claim, and instead announces that he is indeed Odysseus returned. A tearful reunion follows, with Telemachus seeking some proof that he is not being deluded. Odysseus assures him that he is indeed genuinely his father.

> **Task: The reunion simile**
>
> *Why might Homer choose to use a simile that likens the joyful reunion of Odysseus and Telemachus to the bereavement of birds of prey?*

Homer then deploys an unusual simile (lines 212-220) in order to describe their reunion. They cry like birds of prey, vultures or crooked clawed eagles, bereaved when the villagers rob their nests.

Telemachus begins to question his father. How did he get home? Odysseus replies truthfully and instead directs the conversation to the challenges they face. Telemachus then lists the suitors and their origins;

- 52 with 6 servants from Dulichium

- 24 from Same

- 20 from Zacynthus

- 12 from Ithaca with their attendants.

This is a large number, too many for a straightforward confrontation, so Odysseus must use his cunning and guile. Odysseus instructs Telemachus to return to the palace and he himself will come with Eumaeus later. At the appropriate time Telemachus must gather all the weapons present in the hall of the palace and hide them away, all but a few which Odysseus and Telemachus can use. Until then, Telemachus cannot tell Penelope or Laertes of Odysseus' return.

In the Palace (lines 321-450)

Homer now shifts the scene to the palace. Penelope and the suitors hear news of the return of Telemachus. This news is given by a messenger that is sent from Telemachus' ship. Eumaeus arrives at the palace at the same time. The result is that the Suitors as well as Penelope all hear of the return of Telemachus.

The Suitors are troubled by this news. They also witness the arrival of their ship, commanded by Antinous. Antinous is angry and suggests that the suitors need to find a way to discredit and destroy Telemachus; he is becoming a threat. If they choose not to seek out

Telemachus, now hiding in the countryside, then they should instead court Penelope at a distance and abandon dwelling around the palace.

Antinous is replied to by Amphinomus, he advises that Telemachus should not be harmed without a sign from the gods. This is agreed.

Penelope however enters the scene. She is furious that Antinous had tried to kill Telemachus and she confronts him. She reminds Antinous that Odysseus sheltered *his* family and she requests that the other suitors abandon these plots. Another suitor responds. Eurymachus promises that no-one will harm Telemachus. However Homer makes clear that this is a lie. The contrast is clear between the two scenes. Odysseus and his son are united in their plans, the suitors cannot agree and lack unity.

Eumaeus returns (lines 451-end)

The final scene of Book Sixteen is a return to Eumaeus' farm. Eumaeus returns and finds nothing amiss. Odysseus is back in disguise. He does however bring the news that Antinous' ship has returned and this news brings a smile to the lips of both Odysseus and Telemachus.

Task: Eumeaus' news	Task: A Commentary question
Why might the news of yet more suitors arriving be good news for Odysseus and Telemachus?	Read Book Sixteen and answer the question below.
	Read Book Sixteen, Lines 172-201;
	From:
	"As she spoke, Athene touched him with her golden wand..."
	To:
	"Only a moment ago you were an old man in shabby clothes, and now you look like one of the gods who live in the wide heavens."
	How does Telemachus react to his father?
	What does this tell us about Telemachus' character?

Odysseus meets his son

When Odysseus first lays eyes on his son, he does not reveal himself. He leaves it to Eumaeus to greet him as a returning son. Telemachus initially addresses his father courteously, but as a 'stranger', and their first exchange is as one between people meeting for the first time, but Odysseus gauges his son's attitude towards the Suitors and the people of Ithaca.

At Athena's behest, Odysseus steps outside the hut alone, and Athena returns Odysseus to his normal self. This sudden change of Odysseus, from a beggar to king, is effected with no fanfare or announcement. This causes Telemachus to fear and wonder. That he should be so scared and amazed by his father, is something that should not occur between father and son. Telemachus then takes his father's appearance to mean that he is truly a god, and so offers him sacrifices and gold. This shows us how overcome and confused Telemachus is by the moment.

Odysseus and Athena

Odysseus has already received a lot of help from the Gods. This help however, does not diminish Odysseus' status as a hero. Rather because he receives such aid, Odysseus is honoured. The gods do not necessarily support those who are pious, and sacrifices are sometimes ignored by the gods. Instead, the gods only assist those whom they consider able in the first place. Consider Athena's words to Odysseus in Book XVI, lines 168-172; because Odysseus is so resourceful and nimble-witted, she expresses confidence in his abilities to deal with the Suitors and promises to help. Athena is *'eager for the fight'*.

Part Six: Odysseus in the Palace

Part Six: Odysseus in the Palace

6.1 Book Seventeen: Odysseus reaches the palace

6.2 Book Eighteen: *Odysseus, Penelope and the Suitors*

6.3 Book Nineteen: Disguise and Recognition

6.4 Book Twenty: The doom of the suitors

Odysseus in the Palace

Odysseus, disguised as a beggar, heads to the palace in order to assess the situation before carrying out his revenge on the Suitors. Odysseus is treated as entertainment by the Suitors at first. They set him up in a fight with another beggar and they taunt him for his poverty. Odysseus, however, maintains his disguise as he puts into place his plans.

Penelope does not recognise her husband, even in conversation, and through the influence of Athena decides that now is the time to create a test for the Suitors in order to see who is fit to be her husband. Odysseus has a scar and by this is recognised by the old maid Eurycleia and she almost reveals the hero before all is in place. Odysseus prevents this revelation and swears Eurycleia to silence and involvement in his plan.

The weapons are removed from the hall by Telemachus and Odysseus now reveals his identity to two loyal servants who he instructs to help him in the upcoming battle.

6.1 Book Seventeen: Odysseus reaches the palace

In this section we will;

- *Explore the content and style of Book Seventeen of the Odyssey*

- *Consider some of the stylistic techniques used by Homer*

- *Consider some of the linguistic techniques used by Homer*

- *Explore the part played by women in the epic and their position in society*

- *Explore role of slaves and their position in society*

Book Seventeen of the *Odyssey*

In Book Seventeen, Homer begins to draw together several strands of his narrative as the *Odyssey* heads towards its climax. Book Seventeen contains several episodes; beginning in Eumaeus' hut and ending in the palace. In Book Seventeen, Odysseus encounters his enemies face to face; the suitors and their servants. The events that will soon follow are also foreshadowed in Book Seventeen.

Task: Comprehending Book Seventeen

Read Book Seventeen of the Odyssey

Once you have, write brief responses to the following questions;

- *How is Odysseus treated by those he meets in Book Seventeen?*
- *What digressions can be identified in Book Seventeen?*
- *How does Homer foreshadow future events in Book Seventeen?*

Characters in Book Seventeen

The following characters are present in Book Seventeen;

- Odysseus
- Telemachus
- Eurycleia
- Penelope
- Peiraeus, a comrade of Telemachus
- Theoclymenus, a seer and guest of Telemachus
- Eumaeus
- Melanthius, a disloyal goatherd
- Argus, a loyal hound
- Antinous
- Eurynome, a household maid

Book Seventeen: Synopsis

Book Seventeen is one of the longer sections of the Odysseus; at just over 600 lines long. Telemachus and Odysseus both return to the palace. Telemachus travels first and encounters his guest Theoclymenus and is also reunited with his mother Penelope.

Odysseus also travels to the palace. Still in disguise and accompanied by Eumaeus. On his way he meets Melanthius, a goatherd who supports the suitors and gives Odysseus a foretaste of what treatment he might expect at the hands of the suitors. Odysseus also sees Argus, his loyal hound, waiting for his master for twenty years.

Entering the palace, Odysseus faces a hostile reception from Antinous who abuses Odysseus, whom he takes for a wandering beggar. Odysseus holds to his disguise and it takes the intervention of Telemachus, Eumaeus and Penelope for the abuse of Antinous to subside.

The Structure of Book Seventeen

Book Seventeen of the Odyssey can most easily be divided into the following sections;

- Telemachus returns to the palace (lines 1-180)

- Odysseus heads into town (lines 181-289)

- Argus (lines 290-328)

- Odysseus and Antinous (lines 329-497)

- Penelope and Eumaeus (lines 498-end)

> ### Task: The presentation of Telemachus
>
> How does Homer portray Telemachus in Book Seventeen?

Telemachus returns to the palace (lines 1-180)

Homer now begins to shift the scene back to the palace where all the major action that remains in his story will take place. Odysseus and Telemachus, now reunited, continue to conduct a charade in front of Eumaeus. Despite his obvious loyalty, Eumaeus is kept in the dark about the return of Odysseus. Telemachus acts like a stereotypical lordling; he tells Eumaeus to take his beggar-guest into town to beg if he wants; but he *is much too busy* to look after him. Odysseus for his part continues to play the role of the beggar. He will wait awhile before the weather improves before he sets off for town.

Telemachus reaches the palace and is met by Eurycleia, who welcomes Telemachus back home. Penelope too welcomes her son back tearfully but is told, quite sternly, to go to her room and pray whilst he himself goes to fetch Theoclymenus. Reunions and news must wait. The suitors are pointedly ignored by Telemachus. Telemachus now is acting more like a man than a boy; he is more

Task:
Comparing
Books Four
and
Seventeen

Read again
Book Four
334-350 and
Book
Seventeen
124-149

Do you see
anything
similar? Why
might Homer
do this?

self-assured and confident in his own decision making. He heads into town again.

Telemachus' friend Peiraeus brings Theoclymenus before Telemachus and immediately requests that Telemachus take back the treasures he also left with him. Telemachus responds that Peiraeus should keep the treasure for the moment. If anything happens to Telemachus he wants his friend to enjoy this wealth. If Telemachus can solve the problem of the Suitors, then he will claim the treasure. With this Telemachus takes Theoclymenus back with him to the palace.

Once back in the palace, Telemachus now speaks to his mother about his travels. In particular he recalls the words of Menelaus. Homer repeats here the lines he uttered earlier in Book Four. Theoclymenus then interjects with a flat assurance that Odysseus has returned to Ithaca. He knows this to be true because he saw signs on the ship as they sailed into port at Ithaca.

Odysseus heads into town (lines 181-289)

There is now a scene shift. Homer returns to Odysseus and Eumaeus. They set off into town with Homer describing the appearance of Odysseus. If anything, he looks even more like an impoverished beggar than he did before, in rags with an old knapsack and a walking staff.

As they walk, they encounter Melanthius. Melanthius is the opposite side of Eumaeus; were Eumaeus is loyal and generous and kind, Melanthius is foul, cruel and violent to the beggar. Abusing Odysseus verbally, he strikes Odysseus as he passes. This is yet another test for Odysseus. His heroic code encourages him to destroy this peasant upstart, but instead Eumaeus offers a prayer – that Odysseus, when he reappears punish this man for his actions. Odysseus then will have his revenge on Melanthius, but not just yet. They arrive at the palace.

Argus (lines 290-328)

Homer now introduces a small digression. Argus is a hound, the old favourite of Odysseus in the days before the Trojan War. Now Argus, over twenty years old, still waits for his master to return.

Argus has been neglected by the inhabitants of the palace; he is left to lay out abandoned amongst the waste of the palace and his body is plagued by vermin. Argus however recognises his master and begins to wag his tail, though he is too weak to approach Odysseus. It is a pitiful sight that drives Odysseus to tears, but concealing this emotion he asks Eumaeus about the hound. Argus, now that he has seen Odysseus dies, but he has died having seen that his master has at last returned. The digression is a nice touch by Homer. Like the declaration of Theoclymenus, the hound's death is a signal that Odysseus has returned. However, since the hound is neglected, the servants are ignorant of this signal.

Odysseus and Antinous (lines 329-497)

Odysseus now enters the palace and is noticed by Telemachus. He promptly sends Eumaeus to him with food and further instructs Odysseus to beg from the suitors for more. Odysseus makes a round of the suitors begging for food. He does this to establish the character and nature of the men he will soon face in battle. Many of the suitors indeed give Odysseus food, surprised at his appearance, but Odysseus is soon to encounter abuse.

Antinous abuses Eumaeus for bringing a beggar into the palace, Eumaeus replies somewhat forcibly. He does not care for Antinous' opinion, this is Telemachus and Penelope's house and it is *their opinion* here that he respects. Telemachus interjects and asks Antinous to behave.

Antinous seizes a foot stool and brings it out. Perhaps he will offer Odysseus a seat? Odysseus tells Antinous the story he had used previously about being a shipwrecked Cretan, with a slight change. Now he arrives at Ithaca from Cyprus. Seeing that his story elicits neither sympathy nor consideration from Antinous, Odysseus tries a different tack. He insults Antinous as a man without brains.

Antinous' response is violent. He strikes Odysseus with the footstool and threatens to have his servants rip his 'skin to ribbons' (line 480). This response even shocks the other suitors who round on Antinous. The episode shows the audience that the suitors are not all truly evil men, but like Odysseus' crew when they eat the cattle of the Sun; they have already gone too far and are doomed as a result.

Penelope and Eumaeus (lines 498-end)

Penelope now enters the scene, angry at the disturbance in the hall. She prays that Antinous by killed by the Archer god Apollo. She is accompanied by a maid named Eurynome, who supports this utterance. The use of this prayer by Penelope is prophetic, Antinous will indeed be struck down by an arrow; and Odysseus has also predicted the death of Antinous before his *'wedding day'* (line 473).

Penelope asks Eumaeus for information on the beggar. Who is he? Eumaeus tells Penelope what he knows and he also repeats the claim of the beggar that Odysseus will soon return home. Penelope is keen to speak directly to the beggar, but Homer has Odysseus refuse for the moment. Once he is safely in front of the fire hearth after sunset he will speak to Penelope.

Task: The role of servants

Assess the role of the servants in Book Seventeen. What do they bring to the story at this point?

Are they an essential part of the plot in Book Seventeen?

6.2 Book Eighteen: Odysseus, Penelope and the Suitors

In this section we will;

- *Explore the content and style of Book Eighteen of the Odyssey*

- *Consider the use of disguise and deception in Book Eighteen*

- *Consider Homer's use of dramatic irony*

- *Explore the character of Penelope*

- *Examine the characters of the Suitors and servants*

Book Eighteen of the *Odyssey*

The focus of this section is Book Eighteen, and the interaction between Odysseus, Penelope and the Suitors. Book Eighteen very much prepares the way for the climatic events that will soon follow. The primary purpose of Book Eighteen is to prepare for the next stage in Odysseus' *Nostos* (Homecoming). In Book Eighteen, Odysseus quite literally fight his way into the company of the suitors and Penelope not only shows Odysseus something of her cunning nature by tricking the suitors into giving her expensive gifts, she makes an official announcement that she will remarry, which follows in Book Nineteen. This in turn, will lead to the challenge with the bow and as Odysseus taking his revenge.

Task: Comprehending Book Eighteen

Read Book Eighteen of the Odyssey

Once you have, write brief responses to the following questions;

- *How is Odysseus treated by those he meets in Book Eighteen?*
- *What influence does Athena have in Book Eighteen?*
- *How is Penelope portrayed in this book?*

Characters in Book Eighteen

The following characters are present in Book Eighteen;

- *Odysseus*
- *Irus/Arneus, a beggar*
- *Antinous, a suitor*
- *Telemachus*
- *Amphinomus, a suitor*
- *Athena*
- *Penelope*
- *Eurynome, a household maid*
- *Eurymachus, a suitor*
- *Melantho, a household maid*

Book Eighteen: Synopsis

Book Eighteen begins with an argument and a fight. A genuine beggar comes to the palace seeking food and he is most displeased to encounter Odysseus (disguised as a beggar) in his place. Both men square off for a fight. The suitors find this immensely amusing and go so far as to give a reward to the victor; a meal and a seat at the banqueting table from this point forth. After a very one sided fight; Odysseus wins.

Odysseus now has a place in the hall among the suitors and talks earnestly with one of them. Penelope meanwhile presents herself to the suitors and her son Telemachus. She then uses a cunning trick to get the suitors to give her expensive gifts.

Odysseus is still challenged in the hall. He is harassed by a serving girl who he drives away with harsh and threatening words and finally, the suitor Eurymachus taunts and abuses Odysseus before Telemachus and Amphinous calm the situation.

Odysseus enters the palace in Book Eighteen, but the confrontation with the Suitors occurs some books later; likewise the reunion with Penelope is not resolved until book Twenty Three. Homer is carefully manoeuvring each of his the characters into position. Odysseus arrived on Ithaca alone, and then he met and formed a plan with the goddess Athena. He has been sheltered by Eumaeus, before finally re-establishing his relationship with Telemachus. Plans laid, Odysseus literally fights his way into the palace, and the Suitors welcome him in as a result of his fight with Irus.

The Structure of Book Eighteen

Book Eighteen of the Odyssey can most easily be divided into the following sections;

- *The fight (lines 1-116)*

- *Odysseus and Amphinous (lines 117-158)*

- *Penelope (lines 159-304)*

- *Odysseus and the Maid (lines 305-346)*

- *Odysseus and Eurymachus (lines 347-end)*

The fight (lines 1-116)

Book Eighteen immediately begins with a confrontation between Odysseus, disguised as a beggar, and a genuine Ithacan beggar,

known as Irus. Irus, also named Arnaeus in some translations, is a bully who sees an old man begging at the door of the palace, he is determined to drive this old man away with violence, unsuspecting that the old man is actually Odysseus in disguise.

Despite being in disguise, Odysseus is not a man who will be bullied. Odysseus threatens Irus in turn, much to the amusement of the Suitors, who offer dinner to the beggar who can defeat the other in a fight.

Task: The presentation of Irus

How does Homer portray Irus?

What other characters could he be compared to in Book Eighteen and elsewhere in the Odyssey?

Task: The language of the fight

How does Homer portray the fight between Odysseus and Irus?

Something of the potential of Odysseus is revealed when the suitors and the beggar notice Odysseus' physique and Irus suddenly becomes reluctant to fight. He is however forced to fight by Antinous and Odysseus defeats Irus in a brief fight (if such a one sided contest can be called such).

Odysseus is invited to dinner by the Suitors. This incident serves to bring Odysseus into the hall in his disguise and also to be able to speak to the Suitors and learn more about them and what challenges he faces in exacting revenge.

After the fight with Irus, Odysseus is permitted into the hall with the suitors ironically praying that Odysseus *'be granted his greatest wish and your heart's desire'* (lines 113-114). Since Odysseus' greatest wish and heart's desire is to return home and avenge himself on the suitors, they are in effect praying for their own deaths.

Task: Examination style question.

Read Book XVIII, lines 120-157 and 2-4 paragraphs on the following questions;

- How effective is the language used by Homer in warning Amphonius of his fate?
- Do you think the audience should feel sympathy for Amphonius?

Odysseus and Amphinous (lines 117-158)

Odysseus is now handed food and drink by the suitor Amphinous. Odysseus recognises that Amphinous is a kindly suitor and he advises him to leave the palace and go home. Odysseus' words are a warning on the helplessness of men in the face of fate and the gods. He warns Amphinous that Odysseus may soon return and once he reveals his presence, blood will be spilt.

To this warning Amphinous says nothing but retreats from Odysseus, full of foreboding. Homer however makes clear that it is already too late for him. He is doomed to be killed by Telemachus.

Task: Penelope in Book 18

Read Book Eighteen, lines 158-289 paying particular attention to the character of Penelope.

Consider;

- Why does Penelope decide to remarry?
- What motivates her decision?
- What does this tell us about the role of women in Homer's society?

Penelope (lines 159-304)

Homer not only reveals a different side to the suitors through his presentation of Amphinous, he also elaborates on the character of Penelope. She is possessed of her own cunning nature by deceiving the suitors. This deception occurs after the fight between Odysseus and Irus. Athena gives the unwitting Penelope the idea that she should appear before the Suitors;

> *"...with the idea of opening their hearts and enhancing her value in the eyes of her husband and son"*
>
> *Book XVIII.158-9*

Penelope's sudden shift in behaviour is not based on a sudden change in her attitude to Odysseus. She has certainly not decided to remarry out of any disloyalty to Odysseus, and neither has she fallen in love with one of the Suitors. Neither has Penelope been instructed to remarry by her son (Telemachus is the head of the household in the absence of Odysseus).

Homer tells us the reason why Penelope determines at this point to marry again. In lines 250-280, Penelope tells the assembled audience that it was Odysseus' express desire that, should he not return from the Trojan War, she should remarry once Telemachus had reached the age of maturity. Telemachus has now grown to manhood and demonstrated that he is a man by his journey to mainland Greece in search of news of his father. Therefore, in order to obey Odysseus last instruction to her, Penelope must go ahead with her plan of remarriage, because of loyalty to the memory of her husband.

Throughout Book Eighteen, it is clear that Penelope is a woman who is in mourning. She lives with this grief each day, and it is a credit to her strength of will that she can still present an honourable face to the Suitors despite the constant stress of their attention and demands.

In this episode Penelope demonstrates her great love for Odysseus, but is now determined that since Telemachus has reached manhood, and she has surrendered all hope of Odysseus ever returning, that she will remarry. Indeed, at one point, Penelope states that she wishes for death rather than her eternal state of waiting (lines 200-205). Death, it would seem, is preferable to remarriage, but since she is hopeless of Odysseus ever returning, she must go ahead with a second marriage.

This episode demonstrates that Penelope is a fitting wife for Odysseus. Not only is she beautiful, faithful and loyal to the memory and wishes of her husband, she also has Odysseus' deceptive skills. In Book Two lines 89-110 for example, Penelope tries to delay the Suitors with the weaving and undoing of a shroud. This story will also be repeated later.

Penelope is the woman that Odysseus prefers over the beauty and immortality of both Circe and Calypso. Penelope has been praised by Agamemnon in the Underworld as the most perfect of wives. Therefore, it is unsurprising that she is depicted as a perfect wife once Odysseus has returned home.

Task: The role of servants

Assess the role of the servants in Book Eighteen. What do they bring to the story at this point?

To what extent are they an essential part of the plot in Book Eighteen?

Odysseus and the Maid (lines 305-346)

Penelope retires after dominating the hall with her presence. Some serving girls remain in the hall however performing tasks like tending the fire. Odysseus speaks to the maids, they should retire with Penelope and entertain her. He himself will tend the fire. One of the maids, Melantho however decides to challenge Odysseus.

She threatens Odysseus and declares that she hopes that Odysseus gets a beating like Irus did. Odysseus however threatens to report her to Telemachus who would *'hack her to pieces'* (line 349). Like Irus, when challenged the maid Melantho is easily defeated by Odysseus.

Odysseus and Eurymachus (lines 347-end)

Odysseus faces a final challenge in Book Eighteen. The Suitor Eurymachus decides to taunt Odysseus. Apparently Odysseus' disguise involves him being bald. Eurymachus makes a joke about Odysseus' head reflecting the firelight and then offers him work as a farm labourer – not that he will expect him to accept of course as he prefers the life of a beggar.

Odysseus could stay silent; however he responds. If they were to compete as farmhands – Odysseus would far outmatch him, likewise if they went to war against each other, it would be Eurymachus who would be defeated. He calls Eurymachus a bully and like Irus at the beginning of this book, Odysseus has demonstrated how he deals with bullies.

Eurymachus is enraged and hurls a stool at Odysseus. Previously Odysseus has taken the blows of those who strike him, now he ducks and avoids the missile, which strikes a wine-steward. It takes the efforts of Telemachus and Amphinous to calm the situation.

The Suitors as Odysseus' adversaries

What kind of men are the Suitors? Book Eighteen of the Odyssey also serves to flesh out the characters and attitudes of some of the Suitors and it is important that Odysseus has the opportunity to see for himself what kind of enemy he is facing.

As a group, the Suitors are the most dangerous threat that Odysseus will face. Odysseus has been in battle at Troy and knows what it takes to be victorious in battle, but he needs to know how many Suitors oppose him and their strengths and weaknesses. Unlike the Cyclops, whose brute force and savagery was defeated by Odysseus through sheer cunning, the Suitors combine both brutality and cunning themselves. In order to succeed, Odysseus must use both his physical and intellectual strengths (as well as the help of the goddess) to ensure his triumph.

In order to succeed in defeating the Suitors, Odysseus needs to test himself against them before the climactic battle. This is what happens in Book Eighteen. Whilst disguised, Odysseus learns patience and self-control (something that was lacking in his encounter with the Cyclops, and something that his crew failed to learn on the island of the Sun God; to their cost); Odysseus has to tolerate the arrogance and rude behaviour of the Suitors.

Tolerating the mockery and rudeness of the Suitors is perhaps the most challenging trial for Odysseus. Greek heroes did not take kindly to being laughed at; it tarnished their *kleos* and *timé*. A common response to mockery in the *Iliad* is violence. In the *Odyssey* Odysseus must tolerate the Suitors abuse or else risk losing everything.

Homer allows us to see the Suitors in their natural environment. In Book Eighteen, the Suitors are consistently rude and obnoxious to Odysseus when he is disguised as a beggar. The Suitors also demonstrate their total disregard for *xenia*; they have entered another man's house without his permission; they have used and abused his possessions and people as they wish and are now seeking to deprive their unwilling host of his wife by marrying her and making off with the remainder of his property as a dowry.

The Suitors are clearly in the wrong, and Homer presents them for what they are; lawless men who lack honour, and who have made choices to act badly. They are fully deserving of the punishment they shall soon receive. Only one Suitor is shown to express some regret as to his action; Amphonius.

Dramatic irony in the *Odyssey*

Dramatic irony is a deliberate narrative technique used by Homer and is easily identified in Book Eighteen. By delaying Penelope's recognition of Odysseus, Homer creates a series of incidents in which the audience can fully relish the irony. Even though Penelope and the Suitors are unaware of it, the Suitors are abusing and cursing the very man who will destroy them. The use of dramatic irony in Book Eighteen adds to the excitement and anticipation of what the audience knows is coming.

6.3 Book Nineteen: Disguise and Recognition

In this section we will;

- *Explore the content and style of Book Nineteen of the Odyssey*

- *Consider the use of disguise and recognition in Book Nineteen*

- *Consider the use of digression and storytelling in the Odyssey*

- *Explore the character of Eurydice*

- *Examine the character of other servants*

- *Consider the role of slavery in Homer*

- *Examined the role of Penelope in Book Nineteen*

Book Nineteen of the *Odyssey*

This section will focus on the events and characters prominent in Book Nineteen. This section will also touch on some of the language techniques used by Homer in the *Odyssey* such as storytelling and repetition. This section will also explore the theme of disguise and recognition as well as the character of Eurycleia and the role of slaves in Homer's *Odyssey* and the ancient world generally.

Book Nineteen is a book of subtle emotions: Odysseus has borne the insults and mockery of the Suitors, and has maintained his disguise well in the face of this adversity. Odysseus' disguise is tested again in Book Nineteen. Can he maintain his disguise in front of those who know and love him? Can he fool his wife with his disguise, and why is Penelope so insistent about quizzing the 'stranger' for news about the missing Odysseus?

Task: Comprehending Book Nineteen

Read Book Nineteen of the Odyssey

Once you have, write brief responses to the following questions;

- How is Odysseus treated by those he meets in Book Nineteen?
- How does Odysseus treat those who reveal his identity in Book Nineteen?
- How many similes can you identify in Book Nineteen?
- What other stylistic techniques does Homer use in Book Nineteen?

Characters in Book Nineteen

The following characters are present in Book Nineteen;

- Odysseus
- Telemachus
- Eurycleia
- Athena
- Penelope
- Melantho
- Eurynome

Book Nineteen: Synopsis

In Book Nineteen Homer now focuses on two main plot progression points; both focusing on the theme of disguises and recognition. First, Homer has Odysseus and Penelope speak directly to each other, with Penelope unaware of to whom she is speaking to, despite the main topic of conversation being news of Odysseus. Secondly, Homer has Odysseus' disguise revealed; the maid Eurycleia bathes Odysseus and recognises his true identity when she recognises a scar that he has.

Book Nineteen is also a book of storytelling. First of all, there is a story of deception. Odysseus tells Penelope a lengthy story about how this beggar has come to know that Odysseus is alive and will soon return. Secondly, Homer recounts a lengthy digression on how Odysseus acquired the scar that Eurycleia spots.

The Structure of Book Nineteen

Book Nineteen of the Odyssey can most easily be divided into the following sections;

- Hiding the weapons (lines 1-52)

- Melantho (lines 53-99)

- Penelope's story (lines 100-164)

- "Aethon's" story (lines 165-360)

- The Scar (lines 361-466)

- Odysseus and Eurycelia (lines 467-507)

- Penelope's challenge (lines 509-end)

Hiding the weapons (lines 1-52)

Book Nineteen begins with Odysseus and Telemachus concealing the weapons and armour that are usually on display in the hall. The intention behind this is clear; when the conflict does begin, Odysseus is determined that the Suitors will not have ready access to weaponry. Telemachus enlists the help of Eurycleia and Athena too assists by providing light. This momentarily leads Telemachus to forget that Odysseus is in disguise; 'father!...' (lines 35-40). Odysseus quickly hushes his son and sends him off to bed.

Melantho (lines 53-99)

Melantho is a hostile servant who has been encountered earlier. She continues in her abusive attitude towards Odysseus and is evidently ignorant as to his true identity. Odysseus replies with force and although admitting he is a beggar, he warns her that her own current position may change, as his has done.

Penelope is in the hall with some of her maids and she is quick to heap scorn on Melantho, a slave woman who abuses Odysseus.

Penelope's story (lines 100-164)

Penelope begins to ask the disguised Odysseus who he is and where he comes from. Homer interestingly has Odysseus uses the word 'gyne' to address Penelope. This word in the Greek could be used either formally for 'My lady', or informally for 'Wife'. Here then Homer is having Odysseus give Penelope a clue as to his true identity. Homer also has Odysseus use a simile where Penelope is likened to an illustrious king in lines 109-115.

Penelope regales Odysseus with her grief for her missing husband and tells of her ploy with the tapestry (lines 138-164)). This is a repetition of the story told by Antinous in Book Two, lines 89-111) Having done this she asks the *'stranger'* again about who he is and where he comes from.

> #### Task: The language of the chair
>
> *Read lines 53-59. What is Homer trying to do by describing in some detail the features of the chair that Penelope sits in?*

"Aethon's" story (lines 165-360)

Odysseus is now asked for his story. This story is an elaboration of the story told to Athena in Book Thirteen and Eumaeus in Book Fourteen. This time however there are some changes. First of all Odysseus gives a name to his otherwise nameless disguise – his name is Aethon. Secondly Aethon is now the brother of King Idomeneus of Crete. Thirdly he also tells a new story of how he met Odysseus some twenty years ago.

Penelope's response to these convincing lies is tears, and Homer spends some time describing these tears. In lines 204-209 Penelope's tears are likened to snow in another simile. Penelope then tests 'Aethon' as to the validity of his story. She asks 'Aethon' to describe Odysseus, his clothes and his servants. 'Aethon' provides answers that Penelope finds believable and this again causes her grief.

Noticing this grief, Odysseus then retells the story that Odysseus is in Thesprotia, at the sanctuary of Dodona. 'Aethon' also relates that Odysseus lost his ship and crew because they killed the sacred cattle of Hyperion, but that Odysseus reached the Phaeacians and will be back in Ithaca within the month. This news gives Penelope some hope and she now orders a bed prepared for him before the fire.

> *Task: Aethon's story*
>
> *What do you think is the purpose of 'Aethon' talking directly to Odysseus at this point? Do you think it adds or detracts from the story?*

The Scar (lines 361-466)

Eurycleia is the faithful old nurse of Odysseus and a close companion of his wife Penelope. This faithful slave, recognises Odysseus when she washes his feet and notices a distinctive scar that Odysseus gained during a boar hunt.

Odysseus refuses blankets, but does request that his feet be washed. Eurycleia is summoned for this purpose. Eurycleia gives a brief speech regarding his treatment at the hands of the servants and then she declares this stranger looks just like Odysseus (lines 379-381).

Book Nineteen provides an excellent example of the dramatic technique of digression. Beginning at line 393 there is a substantial and lengthy retardation of the plot;

'At once she recognised the scar, the one Odysseus had received years before from the white tusk of a boar when on a visit to Autoclyus and his sons...'

At this point in the narrative, Homer deliberately digresses for two purposes:

- To tell the story of how Odysseus received his scar

- To heighten the drama of the recognition scene

The story of the boar suggests not only Odysseus' physical prowess, but more importantly that Odysseus is *proved* to be Odysseus and the detail of the scar is an excellent way of providing this explanation.

The digression is brought neatly to an end in line 466. Homer finishes as he starts, with mention of 'Autolycus' sons'. The way in which this digression is completed is particularly well described as 'ring' composition, since the digression has returned to where it started.

This scene helps the audience to understand Odysseus more as a character. Odysseus is a schemer and a trickster; a man of disguise and subterfuge. Those to whom he speaks cannot necessarily believe what he tells them. When he does tell the truth, his tales are those of his fantastical and outlandish voyage.

Yet when he lies he is highly convincing and believable. In Book Nineteen it is not his voice that tells the real truth, but his body. The scar is unmistakeable to Eurycleia. No other man could have this distinctive scar, except Odysseus himself.

Odysseus and Eurycelia (lines 467-end)

Homer utilises several sensory techniques in this passage to illustrate the recognition by Eurycleia;

- Touch

- Sound

- Voice

- Sight

First of all references to touch. Eurycleia touches the scar and her shock is apparent. Her surprise is such that she drops his foot, and as a result the metal basin ring out and then spill over, letting all the water onto the floor.

The next device Homer uses is sound. This sudden intrusion of sound in an otherwise quiet and peaceful scene builds the emotional intensity; the sudden clanging noise of metal basin matches the shock felt by Eurycleia.

The third technique Homer uses is voice. Eurycleia's emotion is all too apparent in her words to Odysseus. She calls Odysseus not only her master, but also 'her dear child'. This reminds the audience of the close relationship that Eurycleia and Odysseus once had; after all, Eurycleia was the woman largely responsible for bringing up Odysseus as a child.

The fourth device Homer uses is sight. Eurycleia glances in the direction of Penelope; either Eurycleia suspects that Penelope already knows who this 'stranger' is or Eurycleia is trying to communicate to her mistress that Odysseus is home.

Odysseus' response to this revelation is violent. Eurycleia presents Odysseus with a dangerous challenge and he is quick to act. This highly emotional moment when Odysseus' disguise could be could result in great disaster for Odysseus if the Suitors discover Odysseus whilst he is unarmed and unprotected in his own palace.

Odysseus acts with swiftness and not a little aggression. Odysseus grips Eurycleia by the throat and pulls her close to him, threatening her with death if she reveals his identity. This transformation of the scene from Eurycleia's shock and joy to Odysseus' sudden violence throws both emotions into sharp relief and makes their intensity all the more apparent.

Homer presents Eurycleia's surprise effectively; the clanging metal bowl, the recognition of her master, the emotional words and the death threat pass very quickly and completely unnoticed by the other people in the hall. Penelope might have noticed but is distracted by Athena in another moment of dramatic irony. Odysseus' identity has been revealed, at least to one person, and this revealing occurs almost under the nose of Penelope. She is still completely unaware of just how close her husband really is.

Task: Eurycleia and the scar

Reread this passage, Book XIX. lines 467-481:

From: '*It was this scar that the old woman felt and recognized as her hand passed over it.*

To: *.while with the other he pulled her closer to him.*'

Write a 3-4 paragraph response to the following question;

How successfully do you think Homer builds up the emotional intensity in this passage?

Remember to pay attention both to the language used and the events described.

Penelope's challenge (lines 509-end)

Penelope returns to talk to Odysseus again. She asks 'Aethon' to interpret a dream, to which she already has the answer to. She has twenty geese which an eagle kills; then the eagle returns. Aethon declares the suitors to be doomed.

At the end of Book Nineteen Penelope resolves to test the Suitors as to their suitability to be her husband. In doing so she sets a challenge that only Odysseus would be able to complete. If anyone can do Odysseus' old party trick of stringing his great bow and shooting an arrow straight through a set of axe heads, this is the man that Penelope will take to be her husband. Penelope is determined to be a faithful wife to Odysseus and to follow Odysseus' earlier instructions to remarry if he is absent for too long.

One view is that Penelope has determined that the time for this has come. Odysseus is dead and she must choose another husband. Another view of this incident is that Penelope suspects that Odysseus is already home and uses this challenge to force his to return to her and deal with the Suitors.

Here, Penelope makes final her decision to remarry, despite Odysseus' predictions that her husband is very close by and will come back to take revenge on the Suitors. This trial, a contest with a bride as a prize for the victor, is a common one in Ancient Greek myth; it is a test that only a hero could successfully complete, and is a way for Penelope to decide whom the best of her Suitors is.

It is another dramatic irony that she unknowingly tells her own husband her decision to set a trail of strength and skill to determine who she is to marry. Odysseus encourages her in this plan; so long as he can compete, he can win, reveal who he really is and provide himself with a weapon with which to take revenge all in one go.

Once he hears the plan, Odysseus reassures Penelope again that her husband will soon to make his reappearance, thus paving the way for the time when he will throw off his disguise and take revenge on the Suitors.

The role of slaves in the *Odyssey*

The firm hand with which Odysseus deals with Eurycleia is both a reassertion of his status as master of the household, and also a reminder of this status to his slaves. Odysseus is severe with Eurycleia but he has much to lose and cannot risk detection. Odysseus cannot risk discovery and so Odysseus uses some typical forthright language and violence to ensure that he remains incognito.

However, Odysseus' treatment of Eurycleia is very different to his behaviour to his wife, to whom he is courteous, polite and warm. This is appropriate as Penelope is after all, his host and mistress of the house. She has practised good *xenia* and as a 'stranger' Odysseus must also play his part.

It is Eurycleia's status as a slave that determines Odysseus' attitude towards her. Ancient Greeks were traditionally very conscious of their own and others status. Slave-owning was not something remarkable for mythical Greek heroes; they are part of a noble's entourage and indeed were considered to be the possessions, such as how a modern individual might own a car. Slaves were valuable and could be bought and sold as their masters pleased.

In Book Nine, Odysseus tells his audience how he raided the Cicones, taking plunder and slaves without apology. However, describing the slave-owning relationship in this way does not do it full justice: Homer's *Iliad* and *Odyssey* considers slave-owning to be the norm. Despite this several slaves in the *Odyssey* achieve respect within their specific roles, such as Eumaeus and Eurycleia. The Homeric slaves were possessions, but in return for their loyalty and duty they could expect in return, good treatment, affection and even love.

It is clear that Eurycleia has an essential and valued role to play in the household of Odysseus. Both Penelope and Telemachus have a close and intimate relationship with Eurycleia, and in turn Eurycleia is seen as a leader among the slaves, responsible for the good behaviour of the others. Eumaeus' loyalty to the family of Odysseus is also highlighted.

Together, Eurycleia and Eumaeus represent the household as it should be. By supporting Odysseus and his family and remaining faithful is contrasted the behaviour of some of the other slaves in the household. Melantho for example is a slave who has chosen to side with the Suitors. She is rude and obnoxious to Odysseus when he is in disguise and hostile to Telemachus. After the battle in the hall, Melantho and the other slave women who had been disloyal to Odysseus and his family are executed.

Slaves in the Ancient World

Like most other societies in the Ancient World, the Ancient Greeks practised slavery. Indeed, Greek life and society was inescapably entwined with the practice of slavery. In many ancient Greek cities there were different grades and status of slaves. Some city states, including Athens, had state owned slaves who could serve as public functionaries like clerks and even as a kind of police force. It is thought that Athens, the state that gave rise to democracy, had tens of thousands of slaves; perhaps one out of three of the total population of Athens in the 5th century BC were slaves.

Privately owned slaves included skilled artists and craftsmen who dwelt apart and worked in their own craft shops earning wealth for their owners. They could be leased to others for short periods such as to help build fine public buildings or perform specialist tasks.

Other slaves dwelt alongside the family as servants and tutors to young children; these were known as *'oiketai'* and it is as *'oiketai'* that the slave Eurycleia probably most resembles. Other slaves worked the fields of citizen farmers, or were shepherds to livestock. The most pitiful slaves were perhaps those condemned to work in mines. Their lives were harsh, brutal and short.

Some people in Ancient Greece occupied a position between free individual and slave. Before the 6th century BC, many Athens were 'debt slaves', they had surrendered their freedom temporarily (though this could become permanent) in order to receive finance. Ancient Sparta maintained a huge population of Helots, people bound to work land owned by others. Helots could maintain families and dwell in their own communities, but could also be killed without consequence by a Spartan citizen.

Task: The bow

Reread this passage: Book Nineteen, lines 570-586:

From; *'"However, there is something else I want to tell you that will give you matter for thought...*

To; *...and shoot an arrow through the iron axes."'*

What is the purpose of this passage?

6.4 Book Twenty: The doom of the suitors

In this section we will;

- *Explore the content and style of Book Twenty of the Odyssey*

- *Identify language techniques used by Homer*

- *Consider the actions of the Suitors*

- *Examine the supernatural elements present in Book Twenty*

Task: Comprehending Book Twenty

Read Book Twenty of the Odyssey

Once you have, write brief responses to the following questions;

- *How many similes can you identify in Book Twenty?*
- *What supernatural elements can you find in Book Twenty?*

Book Twenty of the *Odyssey*

As Odysseus' own plans for revenge are nearing their climax, Book Twenty sees the development of the plot towards the climatic events of the subsequent books. As the plot develops the supernatural intrudes into the narrative. The theme of the supernatural permeates Book Twenty.

There is a current of the supernatural that runs through the *Odyssey*. Homer often focuses on the everyday (even when describing monsters), whenever he does emphasise the supernatural it is done with great effect.

Apart from Book Eleven, which is mostly dedicated to the supernatural, the supernatural warnings the Suitors receive in Book Twenty are among the most memorable details of the *Odyssey*.

Book Twenty is one of the shortest in the Odyssey, but it is also a polyphonic episode – despite its brevity many people are allowed to speak by Homer; some praying for the Suitors to be punished, and the Suitors and their supporters in turn guaranteeing by their own words that they will be punished.

By the end of Book Twenty, the scene is set for the final climatic scenes. All the protagonists are placed by Homer in the hall and within reach of Odysseus' revenge.

Characters in Book Twenty

The following characters are present in Book Twenty;

- *Odysseus*
- *Athena*
- *Penelope*
- *Anonymous serving women*
- *Telemachus*
- *Eurycleia*
- *Eumaeus*
- *Melanthius*
- *Philoetius*
- *Amphinomus*
- *Antinous*
- *Ctesippus*
- *Agelaus*
- *Eurymachus*
- *Theoclymenus*

Book Twenty: Synopsis

Book Twenty begins with appeals to the gods. Odysseus converses with, and is reassured by, Athena whilst Penelope prays to Artemis. Come the dawn, Odysseus prays to Zeus for a good omen and is granted two; first of all thunder erupts in a clear sky, and a slave women busy grinding corn prays to Zeus that the thunder is a sign that the Suitors will be punished.

Servants are prominent in Book Twenty. Eurycleia, Eumaeus, Melanthius are all present and a new servant enters; Philoetius, a cow herd, who proves to be a staunch ally for Odysseus.

Task: Character sketches in Book Twenty

As you read, make some notes on the following characters;

- Philoetius
- Amphinomus
- Eurymachus
- Antinous
- Melanthus
- Theoclymenus

Consider how each adds to the plot in book Twenty.

The Structure of Book Twenty

Book Twenty of the Odyssey can most easily be divided into the following sections;

- *Prayers to the Gods (lines 1-122)*

- *The servants arrive (lines 123-239)*

- *The Suitors are doomed (lines 240-349)*

- *The Seer speaks (lines 350-end)*

Prayers to the Gods (lines 1-122)

Odysseus' first thoughts in Book Twenty are thoughts of revenge. He debates with himself whether or not to kill the disloyal servant girls for their affairs with the Suitors. Homer uses several similes in this episode; on lines 14-16 Odysseus' heart is likened to growling like a ferocious dog protecting its helpless pups and again in lines 26-29 Odysseus is likened to a stuffed paunch that twists this way and that in a fire.

He recalls to himself the patience he needed when faced with the challenge of the Cyclops. Athena appears to Odysseus, he desires above all else to avenge himself against the Suitors, but they are many. Athena replies that she will help him in this endeavour.

Penelope wakens and in lines 60-91 she prays to a goddess who has not been present in the Odyssey. This Goddess is Artemis. There are several reasons why Artemis might have been selected by Homer. Artemis is Goddess of hunting and her favoured weapon is the bow. Odysseus will use a bow both to reveal his identity to the Suitors but also to destroy many of the Suitors. Another reason however could be that battle was pending. In Ancient Greece many Greek communities (including Sparta) prayed and sacrificed to Artemis just prior to fighting a battle.

Odysseus too prays. In lines 97-101, he prays briefly to Zeus. As father of the Gods, Zeus was also the god of justice and it is in this role that Odysseus prays. It might otherwise be expected that he pray to Athena, however, since Athena has just visited and declared her support for Odysseus, to have Homer then offer a subsequent prayer to Athena would be at this point superfluous. Odysseus' prayer is answered by Zeus; thunder is heard. This thunder is noticed by the serving women. They too pray to Zeus for the suitors to be punished. Their prayer too is answered by thunder.

The servants arrive (lines 123-239)

Telemachus speaks to Eurycleia on the welfare of their guest. Eurycleia replies that the beggar was well cared for. Homer does not allow either to inform the other of their knowledge (that Odysseus is here in the palace). Telemachus goes into town, whilst Eurycleia prepares the hall and the servants for a festival.

Eumaeus now arrives, driving up fattened hogs ready for sacrifice and feasting. He addresses Odysseus asking after his welfare. As they speak Melanthius arrives. He threatens Odysseus, who continues to keep his silence and restrain himself.

A final herder arrives; Philoetius. He is curious and friendly about Odysseus, and correctly identifies him as a man down on his look, but with the bearing of a king. He offers Odysseus his hand in friendship, knowing nothing about his situation. It is clear from his speech in lines 197-227 that he will be an ally should Odysseus return.

The Suitors are doomed (lines 240-349)

The Suitors enter the narrative at line 240 in Book Twenty and Homer has them deep in discussion; plotting to kill Telemachus. Amphinomus spies an omen that confirms that they will fail in their conspiracy; an eagle clutching a dove. Instead of conspiring, Amphinous instead recommends that the Suitors feast. It is, after all, a feast celebrating the God Apollo (another God armed with a bow and one that offers oracles on future events).

Telemachus has Odysseus seated at the feasting table and orders the suitors to leave him alone as they eat. However, taken aback the suitors continue in their insults. One suitor, Ctesippus, throws a cow's hoof at Odysseus. He misses and Telemachus threatens to kill him if he persists.

'Pallas Athene had fuddled the Suitors' *wits to such effect that they greeted Telemachus' reply with peal after peal of uncontrollable laughter. But before long their laughing faces took on a strained and alien look. Blood was splattered on the food they ate. Their eyes were filled with tears, their hearts with forebodings of grief.'*

Book XX.346-349

Athena now inflicts on the suitors a degree of madness. In lines 345-349 the suitors are overcome by hysterical laughter and try as they might, they cannot stop laughing. It causes them to cry. This is a particularly gruesome sign that the Suitors are doomed; their food is spattered in blood.

Lines 346-357 are some of the most memorable passages in the *Odyssey* because of the supernatural horror that they evoke and these lines also Homer's remind the audience of Odysseus' doomed crew when they slaughter of the Sun God's cattle in Book Twelve.

Odyssues' crew also received a horrific omen in Book Twelve. As soon as they had killed and eaten the cattle of the Sun God, they had committed an act of blasphemy and the gods demonstrated that they were less than pleased. The hides of the slaughtered cattle began to crawl about again, and the meat made the sounds of cattle that were alive. The supernatural horror here, of the revivified cattle and the doom it indicates are echoed here in Book Twenty.

The Suitors are acting irrationally; on a subconscious level they know that this is their last day on earth. Athena had caused the Suitors into a kind of temporary insanity; they laugh uncontrollably, but they don't know why; they are filled with grief and they are crying and again, they do not know why.

The Seer speaks (lines 350-end)

The food they are eating is blood-spattered and one of those present in the hall, a prophet, sees that are the walls of the palace are smeared in blood, a *foreshadowing* of what will happen to them.

Theoclymenus the Seer now speaks out. The Underworld seems to be intruding upon the palace and the suitors are being summoned. There are ghosts on the porch and night and mist have blotted out the sun, clear supernatural interventions.

Having witnessed and announced what he has seen, the prophet Theoclymenus leaves in a hurry. Ironically it is a suitor, Eurymachus, who pronounces that it is the seer that has gone mad. It is even now that the suitors cannot see their own fate. Both the Seer and the beggar should be sold as slaves in Sicily

The horror of these lines is skilfully portrayed by Homer. The future visions of blood-shed have been brought on the Suitors themselves. The blood-covered food is horrific indeed and the blood-spattered walls are worthy of any modern horror.

Part Seven: *Nostos*

Part Seven: *Nostos*

***7.1* Book Twenty One: The Bow of Odysseus**

***7.2* Book Twenty Two: Slaughter in the hall**

***7.3* Book Twenty Three: *Nostos* (Homecoming)**

***7.4* Book Twenty Four: Laertes**

Nostos

Penelope sets up her competition. Odysseus' favourite bow is brought out. If anyone can string the bow and shoot an arrow through a set of axe hoops, then that man is a worthy successor to Odysseus. The Suitors all try and fail to string the bow and Odysseus manages to get his hands on the bow.

The battle, or rather the slaughter, begins with Odysseus, Telemachus and the two loyal servants fighting the Suitors. The Suitors are shot, stabbed and slaughtered by Odysseus and his supporters. Once all are dead the treacherous servants are dealt with in a brutal fashion.

Penelope arrives in the hall and decides to test Odysseus. Odysseus passes the test and the couple are reunited. The Odyssey draws to an end when Odysseus and Telemachus journey to visit Odysseus' father Laertes, who is overjoyed to see his son.

The relatives of the Suitors seek revenge and come to battle Odysseus; however, the gods intervene and peace is made. The *Odyssey* is complete.

7.1 Book Twenty One: The Bow of Odysseus

In this section we will;

- *Explore the content and style of Book Twenty One of the Odyssey*

- *Examine the significance of the bow.*

- *Consider the theme of disguise and recognition in Book Twenty One*

- *Understand Homeric similes and the effects they convey.*

- *Examine the use of flashback in the narrative as a whole.*

- *Explore the role of Telemachus in Books Twenty and Twenty One*

Task: Comprehending Book Twenty One

Read Book Twenty One of the Odyssey

Once you have, write brief responses to the following questions;

- *What stories are told in this part of the Odyssey?*
- *Identify the language and stylistic techniques used by Homer in Book Twenty One?*
- *Which character do you think is most prominent in Book XXI?*

> **Characters in Book Twenty One**
>
> *The following characters are present in Book Twenty One;*
>
> - *Penelope*
> - *Eumaeus*
> - *Telemachus*
> - *Antinous*
> - *Leodes*
> - *Melanthius*
> - *Philoetius*
> - *Odysseus*
> - *Eurymachus*

Book Twenty One of the *Odyssey*

In this section the focus will be the climatic events of Book Twenty One. Odysseus, is revealed as something more than just a wandering beggar. He receives the instrument by which he can deliver the long awaited punishment to the Suitors that have plagued him and his home.

Book Twenty One Synopsis

Book Twenty One has been titled by the translator Rieu as *'the Great Bow'*. This is because the central object, even character, of this episode, is the bow which will resist the Suitors' attempts to string and will be the primary instrument by which Odysseus will take his revenge on them.

The bow is brought forth by Penelope who sets a task. She will only marry a worthy man and that worthy man must prove himself by having the strength and skill of her husband Odysseus. He could string the great bow and he could fire an arrow through the hoop rings of a line of axes. Whoever can repeat this task will be a worthy husband.

The suitors try this task and all fail, Odysseus gets hold of the bow and manages to string the bow and fire an arrow through the axes.

The Structure of Book Twenty One

Book Twenty of the Odyssey can most easily be divided into the following sections;

- *The tale of the bow (lines 1-66)*

- *The challenge of the bow (lines 67-188)*

- *Odysseus seeks allies (lines 189-245)*

- *Odysseus fires the bow (lines 246-end)*

The tale of the bow (lines 1-66)

Book Twenty One begins with Penelope setting up the challenge of the bow and the axes. Homer then gives a digression on the bow and the story of how Odysseus acquired such a weapon.

Book Twenty One has been titled *'the book of the bow'* by many translators of the *Odyssey* because the bow is in some ways the focus; the main 'character', of this episode. The bow was given to Odysseus by Iphitus a Greek from Messene. Within this digression the death of Iphitus is also told; he is slain at the hands of his host Heracles.

In this part of the book Homer uses a simile (lines 50-51) to describe the doors of the storeroom opening like *'the roar of a bull at grass in a meadow'*.

It is notable that the action of this episode revolves around the possession and ability to use of the bow. In many Greek myths, a particular object was used to reveal the identity of someone who is disguised and the ability to either gain access to or use these objects demonstrates that the person doing so is worthy of their use. For example, weapons were hidden under a rock that when discovered would reveal the identity of the hero Theseus to his father. Likewise, in the *Iliad*, Achilles wears distinctive armour, which never knows defeat, until someone else (Patroclus and later, Hector) wear it. The bow is significant in many ways; much like the scar revealed the identity of Odysseus to Eurycleia, the ability to use the bow is another way in which the identity of Odysseus is revealed.

Task: The Great Bow

Read Book Twenty One.

Whilst reading , you should focus on the role played by the bow in this book.

Make a list of the order of the people who hold the bow; consider what kind of language Homer uses to describe their attempts to string and draw the Great bow of Odysseus.

The challenge of the bow (lines 67-188)

The bow starts off in the hands of Penelope, and then passes to Eumaeus, before reaching Telemachus. It is significant that he almost succeeds in stringing it himself, this shows that he is worthy of possessing this object. He *could* string the bow, but Odysseus signals for him to pretend to fail (lines 129-130).

The first suitor to try is Leodes; a suitor who has played no part in the story so far. According to Homer, Leodes is a suitor who hates the behaviour of his peers and after failing, predicts that *'this bow will break the heart and spirit of many a champion here'* (lines 154-155). Leodes is more correct than he knows; the bow will be used to literally *break the heart and spirit* of the suitors – once Odysseus gets his hands on this weapon.

The bow is an object that defeats them. It is as if the bow has a life of its own at this point, since it is unmanageable and unusable in the hands of the Suitors. Strength fails, as do tricks such as warming the bow and using tallow wax to make it more flexible also results in failure.

Task: Examination style response

Write a response to the following question;

"How far do you agree with the view that the bow is more important and significant than the characters in Book Twenty One?"

Your response should include paragraphs that both challenge and support this view.

Odysseus seeks allies (lines 189-245)

As the suitors continue to fail in stringing the bow (they lack the strength of Odysseus and cannot even prove if they have the skill of Odysseus or not), Odysseus himself approaches Eumaeus and Philoetius and sounds them out. If Odysseus was here now would they support him? Both men assure the beggar that they would indeed fight for Odysseus.

Odysseus then reveals his true identity to the pair. If they fight with him they will be amply rewarded and be his close friends thenceforth. He proves his identity by showing his scar. Both men are convinced and begin to help. Philoetius is to block the gates whilst Eumaeus is to return to the hall and bring the bow to Odysseus when he calls for it.

Odysseus fires the bow (lines 246-end)

Returning to the suitors, Homer describes how they have all failed to string the bow. One of the prominent suitors, Eurymachus laments that none of them are a match for Odysseus. Antinous then calls for the contest to be stopped. They should instead feast.

Odysseus now speaks. He wants the bow; and is subject to a torrent of abuse from Antinous as a result. Antinous tells a brief story about the Centaur Eurytion (lines 295-310). Penelope tries to calm the brewing argument but is answered by Eurymachus, who is afraid that if it gets out that the suitors cannot string the bow, this will impinge badly on their *timé* (reputation).

Until now, Odysseus has been silently observing events, safe in the knowledge that it is only he who can string the bow. Penelope now gives her permission for Odysseus to try. If he succeeds he will be given new clothes, a sword and safe passage to wherever he wills. Sensing the climatic events about to occur, Telemachus sends Penelope out of the hall. As she departs, the allies of Odysseus act. Eurycleia locks the doors to the women's quarters, Eumaeus takes the bow to Odysseus and Philoetius bars the courtyard, preventing escape.

The Suitors have no idea of the significance of the bow; this is the object that will kill many of them. Just as they were unaware of the gods' displeasure at their actions in Book Twenty; they laughed madly at the omens in Book Twenty, in much the same way as they laughed at Odysseus and Telemachus, and now they give the bow to the man that will kill them to the sound of laughter.

The bow has gone full circle from its guardian (Penelope) to its future master and owner (Telemachus) to the hands of the enemy, to end up at last with the rightful owner, Odysseus.

Task: Digression in Book XXI

Reread Book 21, and identify an example of ring composition.

Consider;

- What is the purpose of the ring composition here?
- Do you think this digression is effective?

Storytelling and digression in Book Twenty One

Digression, or 'ring composition', is a term used to describe a digression in some part of the narrative before the plot returns to the main storyline. The narrative returns to where it in a circular fashion; hence, 'ring'. Digression is an important technique used by Homer in the *Odyssey* to ensure that detail is added in the digression, but that the main storyline still takes precedence, ensuring that the direction of that is kept moving to its end.

There is a lengthy ring composition from Book Twenty One, lines 9-42; this is a digression on the subject of the bow and its origins. The fact that the digression is of such length indicates the importance of the bow.

Similes in Book Twenty One

There are several examples of Homeric similes in Book Twenty One. Such as the one below;

"While they were talking, Odysseus, master of stratagems, had picked up the great bow and checked it all over.

As a minstrel skilled at the lyre and in song easily stretches a string round a new leather strap, fixing the twisted sheep-gut at both ends, so he strung the great bow without effort or haste."

Book XXI.406-410

The ease and leisure with which Odysseus is able to string the bow indicates his confidence in himself and control of the situation. Now that he has the bow in his hand he can deliver slaughter to the Suitors. The simile is effective in that Odysseus treats this bow- *his bow,* is like a musical instrument. The lyre in the hands of the skilled minstrel is a thing of beauty, so too the bow in the hands of its rightful owner is a thing of beauty.

This simile is suggesting therefore that the bow is more than just a weapon, or a tool of brute force. This precision instrument and the correct use of it, is art. Like the scar in Book Nineteen, the bow is another symbol of Odysseus' rightful status as king of Ithaca. The beauty of the *sound* of the bow in the hands of its true master is another symbol that Odysseus is meant to restore order and rid his home of the chaos of the Suitors

The role of Telemachus in Books Twenty and Twenty One

In Book 20, Telemachus begins to emerge as a much more forceful character. He demands of Eurycleia that Odysseus (still in disguise) is well looked after. He challenges the Suitors, even with violence, if they do not behave themselves. When one of the Suitors Ctesippus, throws a cow hoof at Odysseus, Telemachus threatens to kill him if he repeats the insult. He also declares himself a man to the Suitors, and that he will protect his home.

It is part of Homer's skill in storytelling that he does not neglect Telemachus at this important moment of triumph for Odysseus. It is important to his overall characterisation that, just as Odysseus is the only true king of Ithaca now, so Telemachus is the rightful and recognised heir to his father.

Telemachus has developed as a character through the *Odyssey*. As a young man who is learning the skills and qualities required to be a 'hero' in the mould of his father; such as leadership, confidence and, as will be shortly demonstrated, skill with weapons. Although the revenge is for Odysseus to take, it is important that he is supported by his son in this deed and also by those of his household who are still loyal. So to prove the son's worthiness to this role, he must be shown as competent in his own right; we saw this taking root in the Telemachy and increasingly so since his return to Ithaca.

Telemachus decides to put his own skill to the test using the bow that will one day be his, but not yet. The careful preparations Telemachus makes for the contest slowly develop the audience's anticipation of what is to come. Even the Suitors, who are usually so unaware of events and self-absorbed, cannot help but notice Telemachus.

This bodes well for the future king of Ithaca. There is a feeling of ritual and solemnity as Telemachus attempts to string the bow three times, but fails three times. It is not the right time yet for him to string the bow, since it must be Odysseus' turn now. However, on the fourth attempt Telemachus 'might well have strung it yet' had he not shown his loyalty to his disguised father and let the bow be.

The whole scene is an exciting and touching scene that goes a long way to showing us what kind of man Telemachus is. He rounds off his attempt with some words of disappointment, but he speaks truly when he says that 'perhaps I'm too young, not sure enough yet of my own strength to defend myself against anyone who may care to pick a quarrel with me.' (Book XXI, lines 132-134) He is very right: when he was younger, he was unable to do anything about the Suitors, but now he is very nearly old enough to assume that responsibility of defence that comes with being a king, thus anticipating for us the events of the following book.

Task: Exam style commentary response

Read Book XXI, lines 117-136

From: *"As he finished speaking...*

To: *"Well, sirs, it is now up to you, who are stronger men than I; let's get the contest settled."*

Write approximately 2-3 paragraphs on the following question;

"How successful Homer is at making this episode exciting and tense?"

Points to consider

- Consider the language used by Homer in this passage
- Examine the interaction between the characters in this passage.

7.2 Book Twenty Two: Slaughter in the hall

In this section we will;

- *Explore the content and style of Book Twenty Two of the Odyssey*

- *Understand the theme of justice and revenge in the Odyssey*

- *Understand Homeric similes and the effects they convey*

Task: Comprehending Book Twenty One

Read Book Twenty Two of the Odyssey

Once you have, write brief responses to the following questions;

- *Make a list of the suitors and their deaths. Do they die in order or prominence?*
- *Identify the language and stylistic techniques used by Homer in Book Twenty Two.*
- *What happens to the disloyal servants? Do they deserve what happens?*

Book Twenty Two of the *Odyssey*

This topic focuses on Book Twenty Two, the theme of justice and revenge and the climatic events in the hall when Odysseus and his allies confront and destroy the Suitors.

As has been seen, Homer has carefully and meticulously set up the fluid links between one part of the plot and another Book Twenty Two is no different in this respect. There is a smooth transition from the end of Book Twenty One to the start of Book Twenty Two, where Odysseus throws off his beggar's clothes and finally reveals himself for who he really is. Odysseus is armed with his bow in hand and his son armed with his spear by his side.

Book Twenty Two commences with pace and energy this is appropriate since this episode represents the climax of all of Odysseus' previous trials and tribulations. After much suffering, Odysseus will now finally have his vengeance on those that have insulted his family and abused his home.

Characters in Book Twenty Two

The following characters are present in Book Twenty Two

- *Odysseus*
- *Telemachus*
- *Eumaeus*
- *Philoetius*
- *Antinous, a doomed suitor*
- *Eurymachus, a doomed suitor*
- *Amphinomus, a doomed suitor*
- *Agelaus, a doomed suitor*
- *Melanthius, a doomed servant*
- *Leodes, a doomed suitor*
- *Medon, a herald*
- *Phemius, a bard*

Task: Similes in Book XXII.

Identify at least 3 similes, and consider why you think they are so effective.

Book Twenty Two: Synopsis

Book Twenty Two could be described as a battle, but is perhaps more accurately described as a slaughter. The fighting is distinctly one-sided, and Homer's descriptive language is graphic and brutal.

Book Twenty Two is the climax of the confrontation between the Suitors and the returning king. Odysseus is armed; he has the Goddess Athena by his side and has found worthy allies in his son, Telelmachus and the loyal Eumaeus and Philoetius. The Suitors themselves are doomed and are punished for their actions. Book Twenty Two also sees the execution of the disloyal serving women and the rather graphic torture and death of the disloyal goatherd Melanthus, who had assisted the Suitors in their struggle against Odysseus and his allies.

The Structure of Book Twenty Two

Book Twenty Two of the Odyssey can most easily be divided into the following sections;

- Odysseus reveals himself (lines 1-79)

- Battle (lines 80-141)

- Melanthius (lines 142-202)

- Athena joins the battle (lines 203-241)

- Slaughter (lines 242-329)

- The fate of the servants (lines 330-end)

Odysseus reveals himself (lines 1-79)

This section of the Odyssey begins with the death of Antinous and it is perhaps a measure of this man's crimes against Odysseus and the gods that he gets such an inglorious death. Antinous is shot through the throat whilst he is taking a drink; Homer graphically describing how the 'blood gushed from his nostrils in a turbid jet' (lines 19-20). Antinous dies in ignorance; he does not know who killed him or why and Homer does not even permit Antinous the opportunity to fight and die in battle.

The other suitors have few weapons and no armour; but their first response is to think Antinous has been killed in an unfortunate accident. Odysseus is furious as he reveals his true identity and the words Eurymachus utter infuriate him all the more. He asks for mercy and tries to place all the blame on the dead Antinous. Odysseus refuses to be persuaded, either they should fight or run.

Faced with this situation, Eurymachus demonstrates some courage. He tries to rally the suitors and make them fight.

Battle (lines 80-141)

Eurymachus is the next to die. He is shot through the chest by Odysseus; Amphinous is killed by Telemachus as was foreshadowed by Homer in Book Eighteen. Telemachus now goes to fetch additional weaponry and also armour for Odysseus, himself and the two loyal herders. Whilst he is away Odysseus uses the remainder of his arrows, killing many suitors. The suitors find a new leader, Agelaus.

Melanthius (lines 142-202)

The suitors do try to fight back. The goatherd Melanthius shows more spirit than most of the suitors; he goes to the storeroom and manages to get arms and armour for some of the suitors who now arm. A return trip however is dealt with by Eumaeus and Philoetius. They capture Melanthius in the storeroom. Rather than killing him however, they bind him up and leave him in agony. Melanthius will be dealt with later.

Athena joins the battle (lines 203-241)

Athena now joins the battle. She disguises herself as Mentor (as she did in Book Two). Odysseus knows who she is, but the suitors are ignorant. They threaten the Goddess with violence, which is never a good thing for a Greek to do in battle. 'Mentor' then tests Odysseus; comparing him unfavourably with how he was during the Trojan War. Athena then transforms into the form of a swallow in order to watch the battle from the rafters.

Slaughter (lines 242-329)

The suitors try to fight back. They hurl six spears, but all miss thanks to the efforts of Athena. Odysseus and his allies throw back, killing four suitors. The Suitors try again, but only manage to graze Telemachus and Eumaeus. More deaths follow. The herdsman Philoetius then kills Ctesippus and then gloating over the corpse in the style of a hero exulting in the death of an enemy in the *Iliad*. Athena now instils panic in the suitors, which Homer describes through the combination of simile (lines 298-309) and graphic bloody language. Seeing all the others dead, Leodes tries to surrender. He tells Odysseus of his actions; that he was not a bad suitor. Odysseus however is remorseless and does not spare him.

The fate of the servants (lines 330-end)

Odysseus is still hungry for blood. He notices several non-combatants and it is only through the intervention of his son that the bard Phemius is allowed to surrender. Medon the herald too is allowed to surrender. The battle is over but the killing is not.

Eurycleia is summoned and finds Odysseus covered in blood; affording Homer the opportunity to use another simile. Odysseus now asks her to identify the disloyal serving women. Eurycleia identifies twelve out of fifty. These disloyal servants are ordered to cleanse the hall which they do. Then once they have completed this task they are led out to the courtyard and there are executed by hanging. The women are killed by Telemachus, but he is not yet finished. Melanthius is retrieved and for his hostility to Odysseus and disloyalty he is brutally butchered. He is not hung like the serving girls; instead he is dismembered (lines 474-479).

Once these executions are completed Odysseus purifies the house with fire and sulphur and awaits the arrival of Penelope.

Justice and Revenge in Book Twenty Two

Unlike the *Iliad*, in which descriptions of fighting are plentiful and often without moral comment, the battle scene in Book Twenty Two of the *Odyssey* firmly comes down on the side of Odysseus in the expression of moral judgement. In the *Iliad*, the battle scenes often depict suffering and tragedy for both Greeks and Trojans; here the battle scenes depict the triumphant slaughter of those who are in the wrong.

There are many things that give this away, especially Athena's interventions in the battle on the side of Odysseus. In contrast, no god comes to the assistance of the Suitors. In the *Iliad* however, the gods fight on both sides, until almost the very end.

Odysseus and Telemachus are portrayed not as warriors, but rather as the executors of rightful justice. They are not totally without mercy; it is significant that two of the Suitors' party, their bard Phemius and Medon the herald, are spared. Both are innocent parties but unlucky to be part of the group of Suitors. In the Ancient World heralds were accorded sacred right of immunity and it is a nice touch that Homer also includes the bard in the same category in this instance.

Homer makes it clear in the Odyssey that the death of the Suitors is morally justified. The defeat and deaths of the Suitors represents a triumph of right over wrong. The gods clearly back this outcome since they have ensured the success of Odysseus and his household in the first place.

The moral tone of the Odyssey is established at the very first in the *proem*; the Suitors and the unfaithful maids both choose to act the way they do. They are the ones who abuse the laws of *xenia* and insult Odysseus and his family, and like Odysseus' men after they have eaten the cattle of the Sun God, they can only have themselves to blame for their fate.

Task: An Essay style response

Write a 4-5 paragraph response to the following question;

"To what extent do you consider the punishment of the Suitors *and the maids justified in Book XXII?"*

In your answer you should consider:

- The nature of the punishments of the Suitors.
- The nature of the punishment of the maids.
- Analyse whether you think their punishments are justified in terms of their actions.

Four similes of Book Twenty Two

There are several similes present in Book Twenty Two. Below is a selection with some analysis.

The first simile;

> *"The Suitors were scared out of their senses. They scattered through the hall like a herd of cattle that a darting gadfly had attacked and stampeded, in the spring-time when the long days come in".*
>
> *Book XXII.299-302*

The first simile likens the panic of the Suitors to a herd of cattle. This image is apt as it represents the large number of suitors and how, like cattle when startled by a predator will seek to avoid the threat rather than work together to deal with it. Compare this simile with the fourth one.

The second simile;

> *"But he found the whole company lying in heaps in the blood and the dust, like fish that the fishermen have dragged out of the grey surf in the meshes of their net on to a curving beach, to lie in masses on the sand longing for the salt water, til the bright sun ends their lives. So there the Suitors lay in heaps, one upon the other."*
>
> *Book XXII.382-387*

A second simile is the rather graphic depiction of the bodies of the slain Suitors. In this simile the Suitors are depicted as a fish caught by the fisherman, Odysseus. Like fish the suitors are helpless against Odysseus and once caught in a net their ultimate fate is inevitable.

The third simile;

> *"She found Odysseus among the corpses of the dead, spattered with blood and gore, like a lion when he comes from feeding on some farmer's bullock, with the blood dripping from his breast and jaws on either side, a fearsome spectacle."*
>
> *Book XXII.400-403*

This simile in Book Twenty Two likens Odysseus to a lion. This simile is a common one used by Homer, especially in the *Iliad*. A victorious hero is often likened to a lion when in battle. In the *Odyssey*, the only Greek hero that could rival Odysseus in battle, Menelaus has also been likened to a lion. It is also worth noting that a lion is only usually spattered with gore and blood, after it has feasted on its kill.

The fourth simile;

> *"As when long-winged thrushes or doves get tangled in a snare, which has been set in a thicket- they are on their way to roost, but find a grim reception – so the women's head were held fast in a row, with nooses round their necks, to bring them to the most pitiable end."*
>
> *Book XXII.468-472*

This fourth simile depicts the executed women as small birds that have had their necks wrung. This one is most similar to Simile two, it focuses on small animals (in this case birds) caught and killed by the man made devices of a hunter.

7.3 Book Twenty Three: *Nostos* (Homecoming)

In this section we will;

- Explore the content and style of Book Twenty Three of the Odyssey

- Understand the meaning of Nostos

- Consider the theme of disguise and recognition in Book Twenty Three

- Examine the ways in which Homer reunites Odysseus and Penelope

---

Task: Comprehending Book Twenty Three

Read Book Twenty Three of the Odyssey

Once you have, write brief responses to the following questions;

- Assess the characterisation of key figures in this book
- Identify language and stylistic techniques used by Homer in Book Twenty Three?

Book Twenty Three of the *Odyssey*

This topic focuses on the final two books of the *Odyssey*, examining the theme of disguise and recognition and Odysseus' *Nostos*. This section also examines the interaction between Penelope and Odysseus in Book Twenty Three.

Characters in Book Twenty Three

The following characters are present in Book Twenty Three;

- *Odysseus*
- *Telemachus*
- *Eurycleia*
- *Penelope*
- *Eumaeus*
- *Philoetius*

Book Twenty Three: Synopsis

Book Twenty Three is in many ways the 'end' of the *Odyssey*, despite there being another Book. Odysseus has defeated the suitors and is now to be reunited with his wife Penelope.

The Structure of Book Twenty Three

Book Twenty Three of the Odyssey can most easily be divided into the following sections;

- Eurycleia and Penelope (lines 1-83)

- Telemachus (lines 84-152)

- Odysseus and Penelope (lines 153-end)

Eurycleia and Penelope (lines 1-83)

Book Twenty Three commences with Eurycleia going to awaken Penelope, who rather surprisingly has managed to sleep through the massacre that occurred downstairs. Eurycleia is keen to tell Penelope that Odysseus has returned and killed the suitors; however Penelope is disbelieving, she thinks Eurycleia is insane. Eurycleia persists, stating that the beggar was in fact Odysseus. Penelope starts to believe, but wants to know how this could have occurred.

Eurycleia does not admit to having seen the violence in the hall, she did however see the aftermath and has been sent by Telemachus to fetch his mother. Homer again uses the simile of Odysseus like a lion covered in gore. Penelope instead counters that perhaps it was a god that killed the suitors; Odysseus, if he is still alive is far away. Even now Penelope is suspicious. Finally Eurycleia tells Penelope that she has seen the scar that Odysseus has.

Telemachus (lines 84-152)

Penelope reaches Telemachus and speaks to him, despite Odysseus being nearby. Telemachus asks why she is ignoring her husband? Penelope replies that she will soon find out if it really is Odysseus or not.

Telemachus now speaks to his father. How can they announce what has happened to the people of Ithaca. Odysseus decides on delay, Phemius is ordered to play songs so that anyone passing the palace will think there is a feast.

Odysseus and Penelope (lines 153-end)

Odysseus is bathed and made by Athena to look *'like one of the everlasting gods'*. The scene of recognition is not sudden or easy for either Odysseus or Penelope. This is unsurprising after all that the pair has been through. Penelope is mistrustful of appearances, which is why even after Odysseus' bath, she is unconvinced that her husband has actually returned.

As Homer has shown throughout the *Odyssey*, Penelope has consistently been in utter despair, rejecting the possibility that her husband is still alive; it is understandable then that she should be unable to suddenly accept that Odysseus has returned.

Given the events of the past few years, Penelope is right to be cautious. In Book Twenty Three, she is reluctant to admit that Odysseus is who he says he is, based on appearance and words alone. Penelope is looking for is some sign or action, much like the scar, that will provide the conclusive proof. The statement of Eurycleia that Odysseus is home and that the Suitors are all dead is not conclusive for Penelope; she suspects a god has killed them (lines 1-83). Penelope is still cynical when she first lays eyes on Odysseus, despite the statement of her son and the scenes of carnage that she has witnessed.

When Penelope meets Odysseus, she decides to test him. Success in the test will prove to Penelope who Odysseus is. A conversation about sleeping arrangements leads to a question about the marital bed of Odysseus and Penelope;

"'What a strange man you are,' said the cautious Penelope. 'I am not being haughty or contemptuous of you, though I'm not surprised that you think I am. But I have too clear a picture of you in my mind as you were when you sailed from Ithaca in your long-oared ship. Come Eurycleia, move the great bed outside the bedroom that he himself built and make it up with fleeces and blankets and brightly coloured rugs'."

Book XXIII.173-180

This is another example of dramatic irony. Penelope is attempting to deceive Odysseus, the master-trickster, and it is by Odysseus rising to this bait that he proves his identity.

The trick involves convincing Odysseus that their unique bed, which he built around a living tree, had been moved. Odysseus *is* tricked, insofar as this catches him on the back-foot – he thinks that his great bed has somehow been altered or changed, even though this is not possible.

This outburst proves to Penelope that her husband has truly returned, but more than this, Penelope has shown herself a worthy match to Odysseus. She can be as cunning as him; this deception is the only time in the *Odyssey*, when another human has manipulated Odysseus in the entire *Odyssey*.

Nostos

Odysseus has finally made it home to Ithaca after twenty years away. At the end of Book Twenty Two, Odysseus is depicted as the triumphant hero, victorious in battle and loved by the gods, for whom he is the instrument of retribution and deliverer of punishment to the Suitors. In contrast briefly consider the state Odysseus was in when he is first encountered in Book Five.

> **Task: *Nostos***
>
> Make a bullet point list of ways in which Odysseus demonstrates his desire for *Nostos* (homecoming) in the Odyssey.

The Greek word '*nostos*' means the 'homecoming' or the 'journey home'. This Greek word is the term that is commonly used to describe Odysseus' chief desire; that is, to get home.

It is this driving force that impels him to leave the rather comfortable prison of Calypso, a beautiful, immortal goddess who is clearly happy to have him as a lover. Odysseus is free from toil and want with Calypso, *except* his desire to return home, his *nostos*. *Nostos* then also is the *desire* to return home.

Aside from the battlefield, the home was another of the arenas where a Homeric hero may demonstrate the level of his *timé* and establish his good *kleos*. The home (or more likely, for a hero, the palace) was the place where the hero would store and display his wealth and demonstrate to all that he would honour his family and the gods and deal responsibly with his people. Home is where a hero could display the extent of his *xenia*. It is no surprise that Odysseus should wish to return home, or that Homer would have his hero desiring above all to return home.

Odysseus' new quest

Odysseus must prepare for a new journey however. The dead seer Teiresias told Odysseus in Book Eleven how he might make amends to Poseidon. This quest is repeated in lines 268-284. Although Odysseus has achieved his *Nostos*, it will be short-lived.

Many academics view the natural 'end' to the *Odyssey* at Book 23, line 296. Odysseus has completed his *Odyssey* and succeeded in his *Nostos*. What follows is deemed by many to be an unsatisfactory end to the *Odyssey*. What follows in Book Twenty Three is Odysseus briefly retelling the story of his *Odyssey* in lines 310-343 to Penelope and the loss of his crew.

The next morning Odysseus announces that it his intention to go to visit his father. He does so fully armed and accompanied by his companions; Telemachus, Eumeaus and Philoetius.

The theme of Recognition

It is typical for Homer to delay a particular event in order to increase the impact and dramatic tension. The reunion of Penelope and Odysseus is no different.

Homer *could* have had the *Odyssey* end shortly after Odysseus arrived back on Ithaca, in Book Thirteen. He could have marched up to his palace with Athena at his side and that would have been the end of the Suitors and the *Odyssey*. However, by delaying this reunion Homer increases the tension, ties up loose ends such as the disloyal slaves and, after the slaughter in the hall, the resolution of the entire plot of the *Odyssey*. By doing this Odysseus has not only got home, but also he has got *back* his home, and thus the twin motives driving his *nostos* are completed.

Penelope, however, was notable by her absence in Book Twenty Two. She had retired to her room before Odysseus threw off his rags and killed Antinous and the rest, thus conclusively revealing his identity. The Suitors recognised Odysseus too late and had been dealt with, now it is time for Penelope to recognise Odysseus as her husband.

Recognition through words, not actions

So far, Odysseus has been recognised by his son with the help of Athena, by his slaves with the help of his distinctive scar, and by the Suitors by the decisive way that he dealt with them. Odysseus has *not* used words so much as actions or 'signs' to confirm his identity. In this Telemachus, the slaves and the Suitors have all been brought to recognise Odysseus through *action*.

Odysseus learned much from his encounter with the Cyclops, whilst it was his *words* that persuaded the Polyphemus to eat him last; it was his boastful *words* that revealed who he was to the Cyclops and were to prove disastrous.

Foolishly he shouted out who he was, which enabled the Cyclops to tell his father, Poseidon, who had injured him. After this event, Odysseus is not so rash with his use of words, and instead has learnt wisdom in when to and *when not to* speak. As Odysseus discovered with the encounter with the Cyclops, words can bring about unforeseen consequences.

Indeed, for a man like Odysseus, so accustomed to lying and deceit, mistrusting the uncontrolled use of words and being wary of their power is entirely appropriate. This must be borne in mind when Odysseus meets Penelope in Book Twenty Three.

Task: *The end?*

Read through from book XXIII, line 296 to the end.

In what ways do you consider this a satisfactory end to the *Odyssey*?

7.4 Book Twenty Four: Laertes

In this section we will;

- *Explore the content and style of Book Twenty Four of the Odyssey*

- *Understand the meaning of Nostos*

- *Consider the role of the supernatural in Book Twenty Four*

- *Consider the theme of disguise and recognition in Book Twenty Four*

- *Examine the way in which the Odyssey is ended*

- *Explore the role of Hermes in the Odyssey*

Task: Comprehending Book Twenty Four

Read Book Twenty Four of the Odyssey

Once you have, write brief responses to the following questions;

- *Identify language and stylistic techniques used by Homer in Book Twenty Four?*
- *What supernatural elements are present in Book Twenty Four?*

Book Twenty Four of the *Odyssey*

This topic focuses on the final book of the *Odyssey*. It is a part of the Odyssey that differs greatly from the rest of the narrative and in some ways is inconsistent with what has come before. As a result many academics suggest that Book Twenty Four was a later addition to this epic.

Characters in Book Twenty Four

The following characters are present in Book Twenty Four;

- *Hermes*
- *Achilles, a dead hero*
- *Agamemnon, a dead hero*
- *Amphimedon, the ghost of a suitor*
- *Odysseus*
- *Telemachus*
- *Eumaeus*
- *Philoetius*
- *Laertes, Odysseus' father*
- *Dolius, Laertes' servant*
- *Athena*
- *Zeus*
- *Eupeithes, Antious' father*
- *Medon, a herald*
- *Phemius, a bard*
- *Halitherses, an ally of Odysseus*

Book Twenty Four: Synopsis

Book Twenty Four begins with Hermes escorting the spirits of the slain suitors into the Underworld. They are noticed and commented on by Achilles and Agamemnon, who converse with one of them.

Homer then shifts the scene to the farm of Laertes. Odysseus is at last reunited with his father before shifting the scene again to the town of Ithaca, where the bodies of the dead suitors are brought out to their families. Led by Antinous' father, many Ithacans seek to avenge themselves on Odysseus.

The scene then shifts to the gods. Zeus and Athena converse on events in Ithaca before the scene shifts again back to Laertes' farm and a confrontation between the Ithacans, Laertes, Odysseus and his men. The battle is brief and then a reconciliation is made.

The Structure of Book Twenty Four

Book Twenty Four of the *Odyssey* can most easily be divided into the following sections;

- The Underworld (lines 1-204)

- Odysseus and Laertes are reunited (lines 205-411)

- The Ithacans seek to punish Odysseus (lines 412-471)

- Athena and Zeus (lines 472-488)

- The final confrontation (lines 489-end)

The Underworld (lines 1-204)

Homer (if it is indeed Homer who wrote this part of the *Odyssey*) begins the final part of the poem in the Underworld. Hermes is escorting the souls of the slain suitors to the Underworld and are witnessed by Achilles, Agamemnon and other dead Greek heroes from the *Iliad*. A simile is used to liken the suitors to *'squeaking bats'* lines 5-10.

> **Task: The funeral of Achilles**
>
> Read through from book XXIV, lines 47-97.
>
> Explore the language used in the description of the funeral of Achilles.

Achilles speaks to Agamemnon; he regrets that Agamemnon died an unheroic death at the hands of Aegisthus and Clytemnestra. Agamemnon agrees. He reminds Achilles of the fine funeral that the Greeks gave him when Achilles was slain. What follows is a digression; the story of Achilles' funeral and the fear caused by the sudden appearance of Achilles' mother, the nymph Thetis.

The heroes then interview one of the suitors. The one selected is named Amphimedon. This name has not been mentioned before in the rest of the Odyssey and there is little or no reason for Homer to invent a new suitor at this point.

Amphimedon is known to Agamemnon however and Agamemnon asks what fate brought this group of men into the Underworld. In lines 120-148 Amphimedon recounts the story of Penelope weaving a funeral shroud for Laertes (this story has already been told in Book Two and again in Book Nineteen). The suitor then recounts how Odysseus and Telemachus destroyed the suitors in the hall; this lengthy repetition is for the benefit of Agamemnon and the others.

Agamemnon rejoices at this news. He is happy that Odysseus has overcome his enemies and been reunited with his loyal wife. He compares Penelope favourably to his wife Clytemnestra; she will win fame and renown for her loyalty. *His* wife on the other hand will be infamous and her acts destroyed the reputation of all women.

Odysseus and Laertes are reunited (lines 205-411)

> **Task: The deception of Odysseus**
>
> Read through from book XXIV, lines 259-315.
>
> Why do you think Homer has Odysseus lies to his father at this stage of the story? How effective do you think this episode is?

Odysseus now visits his father on his farm. Finding the house empty, he orders Telemachus and the others to prepare a meal and he himself seeks out his father. Laertes is dressed as a peasant; scruffy and dirty. Odysseus pities the sight but this does not stop him from employing his native cunning. He twits his father; *whose serf is he?* (lines 257-260).

Odysseus also then decides to tell his father a lie. He tells Laertes that he is a wealthy stranger seeking out Odysseus. He says that he saw Odysseus some five years ago. This story causes Laertes such grief that Odysseus breaks off his deception and reveals who he is.

Laertes asks for proof. Is he really his son? Odysseus then shows his father the scar that has proved his identity to Eurycleia and others. He also mentions the orchard and the trees that his father gave him. Again this is odd. No hero in the Odyssey or Iliad eats fruit. However, in the Ancient World landownership was an important part of wealth and wealthy Greeks often demonstrated their wealth through the fruit of their orchards.

This is proof enough for Laertes who is now reunited with Odysseus. They eat and Odysseus is also reunited with Dolius, Laertes loyal friend and servant.

The Ithacans seek to punish Odysseus (lines 412-471)

Homer now shifts the scene to the town of Ithaca. The bodies of the suitors are brought out of the palace and given to their families. Many affected are angry. Not only has Odysseus lost the flower of the Ithacan army in the Trojan War, he now kills the best of those that remained. Antinous' father Eupeithes calls for revenge.

Medon and Phemius urge restraint; an immortal, the Goddess Athena fought alongside Odysseus. Halitherses, who was last seen in Book Two, he reminds them of the actions of the suitors. Halitherses' speech has some effect. Half of the Ithacans assembled go home, the other half arm and seek to fight Odysseus.

Athena and Zeus (lines 472-488)

Homer then digresses the narrative briefly with a conversation between Zeus and Athena. Zeus instructs that peace be made and Athena goes to intervene.

The final confrontation (lines 489-end)

Odysseus is warned of the approach of the angry Ithacans. He calls for his arms and armour and all the men present gear themselves for war. They are joined by Athena, in disguise as Mentor. Odysseus, Laertes and Telemachus exult at the thought of demonstrating their power and courage. Athena encourages Laertes who strikes the first blow; a spear throw that kills Eupeithes. As Odysseus and Telemachus attack, Athena calls on them to stop. The Ithacans drop their weapons and turn to run and Odysseus attacks them again. It takes a direct command from Athena and a thunderbolt from Zeus to stop him. Peace is then made.

Many readers have found the final book of the *Odyssey* as somewhat anti-climactic. After the satisfying resolution of Books Twenty Two and the first part of Book Twenty Three the remainder comes across as clumsy and unconvincing for many.

Task: The final book

Write a response to the following essay style question;

To what extent do you agree with the view that the final book of the *Odyssey* adds nothing to the narrative of the story?

Hermes in the *Odyssey*

Perhaps the most defining story of Hermes, the son of Zeus and the nymph Maia, is the story that on the day of his birth; he not only stole the cattle of Apollo and successfully hid them from him, he also invented a musical instrument. Hermes then, is a very versatile God.

Given the events of his first day, it is no surprise that Hermes serves many roles as a God in both the Greek and Roman Pantheons. He is a messenger but Hermes is also the god that guides shepherds. He is a patron of children, the god of prosperity and also Hermes is the god that leads the spirits of the dead to the Underworld.

Hermes in Book Five

Hermes plays an important, albeit brief, role in Book 5 of the *Odyssey*. It is he who is sent by Zeus to the goddess Calypso to instruct her that she must allow Odysseus to leave her island. Although Calypso is not entirely happy about the command, she submits to the will of Zeus. Homer describes Hermes as follows;

> 'From the upper air he dropped to the Pierian range, and from there swooped down on the sea, and skimmed the waves like a sea-gull drenching the feathers of its wings with spray as it pursues the fish down fearsome troughs of the unharvested deep'
>
> *BookV.50-54*

In this Book of the *Odyssey*, Hermes is acting as the messenger of Zeus. In this particular simile Homer likens Hermes to a sea gull, with the swiftness of Hermes elaborated by this comparison. His speed is as divine and his graces of movement are all pronounced in this passage.

Hermes in Book Ten

Although Hermes has already made a brief appearance in Book Five of the *Odyssey*, his intervention in Book 10 is perhaps even more important. At this point in the *Odyssey,* Odysseus has learned that the witch-goddess Circe has transformed some of his men into pigs. Alone, Odysseus does not stand much chance against Circe. However, on his way to confront Circe, the god Hermes appears to him, recognisable at once to the hero. Hermes gives Odysseus a magical herb, moly that will protect him against Circes' magic and also instructs him how to turn Circe from foe to friend;

When Circe strikes you with her long stick, you must draw your sword from your side and rush at her as though you mean to kill her. She will shrink from you in terror and invite you to her bed. You must not refuse the goddess' favours if you want her to free your men and look after you'.

Book X.294-297

In this passage Hermes is not acting as a messenger for Zeus. Instead, Hermes is acting on his own behalf, as a patron, a protector of the hero. This does however raise a few questions;

Why has Hermes not helped before when he helps here? Secondly, and more importantly, why has Athena not assisted Odysseus at this point? The reason why Homer has Hermes intervene at this point, and not Athena, could be down to the instructions that Hermes gives Odysseus. Hermes instructs Odysseus not only to threaten Circe, but to sleep with Circe in order to obtain both the release of his men and guidance in his journey. If Athena had instructed Odysseus to do this, she would be acting outside of her role as a virgin goddess

Task: The role of Hermes in the *Odyssey* and the language of Homer

Reread the passage in Book V.43-57 and Book X.277-307 and then write a 4-5 paragraph response to the following question;

How effectively does Homer convey Hermes' supernatural qualities in these passages?

Remember to pay attention both to the language used (including similes) and the events described.

Examination style questions, Translations and Further Reading

Examination style questions

Practice Papers may be obtained free of charge from the examination boards.

Depending on the examination board;

Go to either;

www.aqa.org.uk

or

www.ocr.org.uk

Use their search facility to find 'GCE Classical Civilisation'

Each examination board offers additional materials including the subject specification, past papers and reading lists.

Each examination board also uploads a mark scheme and notes for examiners. These are extremely useful as they reveal what elements are being assessed in any particular question as well as potential pitfalls to avoid.

Sometimes, due to copyright reasons, the examination boards do not display the Section A commentary passages.

Below is a selection of thematic exam style questions;

1. Odysseus always acts and behaves as a hero should in the *Odyssey*? To what extent do you agree?
2. Assess the importance of the role of the Gods in the *Odyssey*?
3. To what extent is the practice of *xenia* the main reason why Odysseus reaches home?
4. 'Without the assistance of slaves and servants, Odysseus would never succeed in overcoming the suitors'. To what extent do you agree with this view?
5. 'Odysseus' greatest talent is for deception'. To what extent do you think this is true in the *Odyssey*?

Translations of the *Odyssey*

The 'set text' recommended by both AQA and OCR examination boards is the following;

Homer, *Odyssey*. Translated by E.V.Rieu, Penguin, revised edition 1991 (reprinted 2003)

Unless otherwise stated the quotes and excerpts used in this guide are drawn from this version.

However, OCR do state that ANY complete translation of Homer's Odyssey may be used to study for this unit.

Another excellent translation is;

Homer, *Odyssey*. Translated by R.Fagles, Viking Penguin, 1996.

Free versions of the Odyssey can be obtained from;

The Perseus digital Library

www.perseus.tufts.net

Both Kindle and iBooks also offer free versions of the Odyssey

---

Further Reading

Below is a brief selection of books on the *Odyssey*

Boardman, J., Griffin, J. & Murray, O. *The Oxford History of the Classical World.* (Oxford: Oxford University Press) 1986

Dawe, R.D The Odyssey: Translation and Analysis (Lewes Book Guild) 1993

Finley, M.I. *The World of Odysseus.* (Hammondsworth: Pelican Books) 1979

Griffin, J. *Homer: The Odyssey.* (Cambridge: Cambridge University Press) 1987

Jones, P.V. *Homer's Odyssey: A Companion to the Translation of Richmond Lattimore.* (Bristol: Bristol Classical Press) 1988

Rubens, B & Taplin, O An Odyssey around Odysseus (London: BBC Books) 1989

Wace,A.J.B & Stubbings, F.H. *A Companion to Homer.* (London: London) 1962

About Athena Education Online

Athena Education Online are a specialist team of professional course writers based in Lincolnshire, UK. All course writers are specialists in their area and are all are experienced teachers and lecturers as well as experienced examination assessors for the main examination boards, including AQA, OCR, Edexcel and CIE.

About the Author

P Kenney is an experienced, course writer, college lecturer and tutor and examiner for several examination boards. A graduate of the University of Wales and postgraduate of Nottingham University in Classics, History and Archaeology. He has written critical guides on a range of historical and literary texts.

About the Editor

T Kenney is a teacher, examiner and moderator in English Literature and English Language and Literature. She is a postgraduate of Cambridge University and the Open University with a MA in Literature. She has written critical guides for a range of poetry, prose and drama texts.

Terms and Conditions of Use

Thank you for purchasing this product.

By purchasing this product you acknowledge that we the producers of these materials are not affiliated with any educational institution, that this product is authorised by, sponsored by, or affiliated with any educational institution.

Use of this product does not ensure any expected exam grade of anyone owning or using this product. Neither do Athena Online Education guarantee that this product is affiliated with, or suitable for, any particular examination board or examination unit, however Athena Online Education will strive to ensure that all of its products match as closely as possible the qualification for which it is intended to support.

Copyright Information

The materials contained within this product may not be incorporated into another body of work without prior reference to, and acknowledgement from Athena Online Education.

Whilst every effort has been made to ensure that the information provided in this product is up to date and accurate, no legal responsibility is accepted for any errors, omissions or statements which may otherwise mislead. It is the policy of Athena Online Education to attempt to obtain permission for any copyright material contained within their publications.

All images included in this product were sourced from the author's own records, wiki commons and other public domain material. Where an error has occurred Athena Online Education will happily rectify or remove images not in the public domain if contacted.

Disclaimers

This product is designed to be a supplement to learning only.

Although it may incorporate practice questions and material designed to follow the content of an examination specification. These learning materials are in no way an attempt to predict future examination materials and should not be treated as such. Athena Online Education does not make warranty as to future results users may obtain in examinations from the use of this product. Likewise, Athena Online Education does not make warranty as to the accuracy, content or reliability of the product. It is intended that this product be used appropriately and at the users own discretion. It is the user's responsibility to assess the suitability of this product to their own circumstances.

Athena Online Education is not affiliated with any examination board in any way nor is this product authorised, associated with, sponsored by or endorsed by, these institutions unless explicitly stated on the front page of the product.

Links to, and references to, other websites and resources are provided where appropriate. Athena Online Education is not responsible for the information of these sites and links and cannot guarantee, represent or warrant that the content contained on any website or resource are legal, accurate or inoffensive. Links to, and references to, websites and resources should not be taken to mean that Athena Online Education endorses these websites and resources in any way.

Made in United States
North Haven, CT
16 January 2023

31145437R00153